Praise for John Barth

"Barth's earlier accomplishments amount to a watershed for the country's fiction, a landmark in what's known as Postmodernism. . . . As Barth's work matures, its elements of experiment take us further from the ordinary."
—John Domini, *LitHub*

"Every sentence he writes either looks at itself askance or ushers in a following sentence that will perform the task. In his fascinated commitment to the art—and to the criticism—of storytelling, he has no rival."
—William Pritchard, *New York Times*

"John Barth has spent most of his allotted era watching our wheels spin with a coolly detached, not unamused gaze. He doesn't ignore or eschew change, but he takes a wider view. He is Heraclitean to the core. . . . If, as Nabokov wrote in the Afterword to Lolita, art is kindness, then John Barth embodies art every bit as much as anyone ever has."
—James Greer, *LA Review of Books*

Other Books by John Barth

John Barth

POSTSCRIPTS
(OR JUST DESSERTS)

Some Final Scribblings

DALKEY ARCHIVE PRESS
Dallas / Dublin

Copyright © 2022 by John Barth

First edition
All rights reserved

PB: 978-1-62897-446-1
Ebook: 978-1-62897-473-7

Library of Congress Cataloging-in-Publication Data: Available.

Interior design by Anuj Mathur

Dalkey Archive Press

www.dalkeyarchive.com
Dallas/Dublin

Printed on permanent/durable acid-free paper.

For Shelly, *como siempre!*

Beloved life-partner, editor of first resort, moral compass, dedicatee of every book I've published since our marriage in 1970, and all-round *sine qua non.*
1001 thanks, dear Shelly!

FOREWORD AND ACKNOWLEDGEMENTS

For the first decade of my publishing career, my genre of choice was the novel. With four of them under my belt, I then tried short stories and novellas, in both cases inclining toward related series—*books* of stories, *triads* of novellas—rather than discrete, stand-alone items, and often returned to the full-length-novel genre between those story-series and novella-triads, while also publishing several collections of essays. Now in my nineties, having perpetrated eleven novels, two novella-triads, four short-story series, and three essay collections, I find myself attracted to the even shorter form of mostly one-page *jeux d'esprits*, with the title "Postscripts" and the subtitle "Just Desserts."

Certain names—especially Odysseus and Scheherazade—turn up repeatedly in these essays, having been of particular importance to my writing. Even a phrase or sentence in one essay may recur in another, written years later. By way of apology (or whatever) I quote Walt Whitman: "Do I repeat myself? Very well, then: I repeat myself." See the little essay "Navigation Stars," *infra*—and bear with me, patient reader!

A number of these tidbits—"Harley Guy," "Cat Man," "*Chrysaora Quinquicirrha*," "The Sirens' Song," "Facts of Life: The Python," "The Second Person," "Dermatology," "Weekly Specials!," and "Bonus Time"—first appeared in the quarterly *Fiction*, "Missy" in *Iowa Review*, "Dead Ringer" in *Threepenny Review*, "Out of the Cradle" in *Granta*, and the tributes to Donald Barthelme, Robert Coover, and Stephen Dixon in their respective Festschrifts. My thanks as always to Jacqueline Ko and her colleagues at The Wylie Agency for steering these pieces into print both individually and now in book form.

Bon appetit!

Contents

Postcsripts

SELF-EXPLANATORY HAIKU

Five beats in Line One,
Seven beats in the second,
Five beats in the third.

EPIGRAPHICAL HAIKU

These are my Postscripts
Or Just Desserts, not *entrées*.
Dig in, friends: Enjoy!

IN THE BEGINNING WAS
THE (SPOKEN) WORD*

Just as the oral tradition in literature antedates the written (not to mention the invention of print), so the *sayings* of such iconic sages as Socrates, Jesus, Buddha, Mohammed, and Confucius precede—sometimes by centuries—their inscription. None of the above-mentioned was illiterate: All of them could (and did) read and write. Interestingly, however, none chose to personally inscribe the teachings for which they are revered, preferring instead to leave that task to their disciples, or even the disciples of the disciples of their disciples. Plato recorded the dialogues of his mentor Socrates, who objected to writing lest it take the place of memory and the give-and-take of argument. Matthew, Mark, Luke, and John set down the gospels of Jesus (but the earliest *extant* texts date from the second century CE). Luke speaks of Jesus *reading* from the Book of Isaiah in the synagogue of Nazareth, and John tells of Jesus *writing* something (in the dirt, with his finger) that persuaded the scribes and Pharisees not to stone to death the woman

---

* Essay written in 2013 for a lecture; here published for the first time.

4

taken in adultery—though his famous admonition "Let him who is without sin cast the first stone" was spoken, not written. The Buddha as a youth was well educated by the standards of the time and so presumably could read and write, but his teachings, like those of Socrates and Jesus, were recorded by his followers, as were those of the also-literate Confucius (Mohammed/Muhammad's literacy is a matter of dispute, as is the authorship of the *Koran*). The "wisdom of the sages"—the Ten Commandments, the teachings of the Buddha and Confucius, the Lord's Prayer, the Rosary—was often recited communally, a safeguard against error, but practical only with short texts: their *sayings*. The bards, of course, could recite over a period of days such book-length epics as the *Iliad* and *Odyssey*; but they were professionals, who no doubt shortened, lengthened, modified, and embellished their deliveries to suit the occasion. Scheherazade famously *tells* King Shahryar her entertain-me-or-die stories over 1001 Arabian nights: Some of them require more than one night to complete, especially those that artfully contain secondary and even tertiary tales within the primary one, and when she finishes one story she immediately begins the next, interrupting it *in medias res* at the crack of dawn so that the king will spare her life for the sake of its continuation. No doubt he soon becomes aware of her strategy, but he doesn't acknowledge it until the end, when he abandons his murderous policy, marries her for the sake of her stories and the three children that he has fathered upon her over the span of their telling—and then commands her to *recollect and repeat* all those stories for official inscription! We are not told how she manages *that* Herculean labor: a much more considerable task than their original incremental recitation, though mercifully not to be performed under threat of death.

If the oral transmission of texts is famously subject to error (e.g., the old parlor-game "Gossip," in which a not-all-that-complicated written message is transmitted by ear-to-ear whisper down a line of ten or twelve people, the last of whom recites aloud its by-then-garbled version to the company's amusement), it's to be noted that writing wasn't infallible either before the invention of print, and that copyediting glitches can still be a nuisance: I've sometimes found small errors in my printed books even after careful proof-readings by their author, his sharp-eyed wife, and his publisher's excellent copyeditor.

In my decades in academia as an undergraduate, graduate student, professor, and professor emeritus, I've attended hundreds of readings by poets and fiction-writers, as well as delivering hundreds myself all over the US and in numerous other countries until I retired both from teaching and from the lecture/reading circuit, and I've come to appreciate the differences between the spoken and the written word. While it's never uninteresting to hear prose and poetry that one admires read aloud by its author, not every good writer is *ipso facto* an effective, *authoritative* reader of her/his work, or even necessarily a good selector of which texts make an effective program of readings. In my mind's ear, so to speak, I can still hear Dylan Thomas beautifully incanting, "*Do not go gentle into that good night. Rage, rage against the dying of the light,*" and Robert Frost declaring quietly, "*Two roads diverged in a wood . . . I took the one less traveled by, and that has made all the difference.*" Donald Barthelme and John Hawkes, both of whom I was several times privileged to share platforms before their untimely deaths, were very different but equally impressive readers of their own work: Hawkes impassioned, Barthelme programmatically unhistrionic. Them too I can still hear, with pleasure, whenever I read their sentences. As for indifferent or downright boring readers of their own work . . . I won't name names.

Back in the "High Sixties" of the twentieth century, some more or less avant-garde writers (myself included) thought it "cool" to accompany their readings with visual or other gimmicks. I recall an extended "reading" by Richard Brautigan that consisted of his starting a reel-to-reel tape recording of his short prose pieces, then withdrawing to a projection booth in the rear of the hall to show protracted (and not evidently relevant) slides of a comma, a semicolon, or a period, and finally emerging from that booth to declare, "There you have it, folks: The Twentieth Century!"—to which a bored audience-member beside me grumbled, "Yeah: about 1913." And I myself was guilty back then of such gimmicks as brandishing placards of left-and-right quote-marks and quote-within-quote-within-quote-marks while reading "Menelaiad," a nest of tales-within-tales-within-tales from my 1968 collection *Lost in the Funhouse* (subtitled *Fiction for Print, Tape, Live Voice*).

What fun, the Terrible Twentieth: two World Wars, the Great Depression, the Cold War and the Korean and Vietnam Wars; movies, television, and the internet; automobiles, airplanes, and computers; the A-bomb and the H-bomb; satellites and ICBMs; Dada and Surrealism; Modernism and Post-Modernism! And now the Twenty-First!

When such in-your-face innovation has perhaps come

to feel a bit . . . *passé?* Just as those of us nowadays who
still read books for pleasure may prefer actual *books*, with
covers and bound pages, to ebooks on a screen, we may
when reading fiction prefer *stories* containing a beginning, a middle, and an ending—even if (as Horace recommended way back when) those stories begin *in medias
res.* My own productions, I notice, became less obviously "experimental" after the 1960s, although of course
every story, every essay, indeed every sentence, is a sort of
experiment: an attempt (as the word "essay" implies) to
render ideas, notions, hunches—inspirations!—into language. The "experimental" aspect of those later works of
mine is limited mainly to their reorchestration of such
once-popular genres as the epistolary novel (in my 1979
novel *LETTERS*) and the frame-tale cycle (*The Tidewater
Tales, On with the Story,* and *The Book of Ten Nights and a
Night*): the stories themselves are relatively traditional in
their structure and presentation.

So? Does that mean that their author has become, in
his old age, more *conventional?* Not impossibly—at least
in that he perhaps appreciates and respects the conventions of traditional storytelling more than he did as a
younger practitioner. But among those traditions is the
tradition of innovation, of *un*conventionality, as in the
visual/typographical playfulness of Laurence Sterne's
eighteenth-century *Tristram Shandy* and Denis Diderot's
Jacques the Fatalist and His Master, or those over-the-
top catalogues in François Rabelais' sixteenth-cen-
tury *Gargantua and Pantagruel*; likewise the tradition
of transcendently mocking Tradition, as in Cervantes'
spoof of generic chivalry-novels in *Don Quixote,* often
regarded as the first "modern novel." My own current

project-more-or-less-in-the-works is (anyhow aspires to be) a volume of short pieces entitled *Postscripts* (and subtitled *Just Desserts*)—mostly non-narrative quick takes rather than stories—but I quite respect, even honor, the *conventions* of storytelling, without which there would be nothing to innovate from. The lead-off piece in my 1968 collection *Lost in the Funhouse* is a Möbius strip reading ONCE UPON A TIME THERE WAS A STORY THAT BEGAN: when scissored out and assembled (i.e., head joined to tail, a circle with a twist: an apparently three-dimensional thing that in fact has only one surface and one edge) its ten words become both the shortest story ever told—or at least begun—and the longest, as there is no end to it, nor a middle, nor even a real beginning, only the announcement that one is pending.

Are we having fun yet? It seemed so, back in that century's turbulent sixties and this author's fertile thirties: fifty years later I still recall with pleasure those formal high jinks, even if I find myself now rather less inclined to them at the writing-desk. Those were the days! . . .

And these are these, and I return to my subject: the spoken versus the written word; story-*telling* versus story-writing; story-*hearing* versus story-reading. The literal meaning of inspiration, the source of art, is "being breathed into" by one's muse: a figurative CPR. The Homeric bards began their epic recitations by commanding (or ritually imploring, probably after taking a deep breath), "*Sing*, O Muse, of [the fall of Troy, the wanderings of Odysseus or Aeneas, whatever] . . ." Most writers, likewise, commence their work-sessions with some sort of preparatory ritual, or at least routine: my own, as I've noted elsewhere, consists of refilling my thermal mug with breakfast coffee, partially closing the door to my study (i.e., interrupt me if you must, but *only* if), inserting wax earplugs even though the house is normally quiet (a habit carried over from pre-empty-nest days), refilling my fountain pen whether or not it's dry, opening my old and very shopworn three-ring loose-leaf binder, reviewing whatever draft-in-progress or my notes thereto—in the best case, a draft left off when the going was good, with a scribbled hint of what's to come next—and then, Muse willing, carrying on for some three hours-worth of further sentences and paragraphs, getting up every hour or so to stretch my legs or otherwise relieve myself. At eleven o'clock or thereabouts I cap my pen, turn from writing-desk to word-processor, computerize the morning's output for subsequent editing and revision, unplug my ears, check the e-mail, and exit the room for lunch. If I return to it later that day, it will be for correspondence, accounting, or other deskwork, not for intercourse with Ms. Muse.

The product of those sessions, if and when it finds its way into print, differs from oral transmission in at least three important respects. The printed word is a silent, relatively non-sensory transaction between author and individual readers: while paper-quality, type-font, book-bindings, and the like may be of varying quality and appeal, the story is the story apart from them, and its printed transmission is anesthetic compared to watching and hearing a movie, a stage-play, or even a live reading. On the other hand, a printed text has the considerable advantages of being 1) *interruptible* (you can stop reading at any point, even in mid-sentence, bookmark the page, and return to it later or not, as you could scarcely do in the oral tradition unless you were the Sultan and could say to Scheherazade, "That's enough for tonight, thanks; on with your story tomorrow"), 2) *referable* (you can go back a few paragraphs or pages to remind yourself where you left off reading yesterday, or exactly when—to use Chekhov's famous image—the author hung that rifle on the wall in Act One that now gets fired in Act Three), and 3) *mass-reproducible*: advantages available to spoken texts only since the invention of sound-recording, and limited there for the most part to relatively short texts, though of course there are also "audiobooks." I myself can't imagine *listening* to a novel; perhaps I'd feel otherwise if for one reason or another I were unable to read, but in that event, I suspect I'd prefer a short story, deliverable "in a single sitting," as Edgar Allan Poe recommended. To read silently the script of a stage-play or film is obviously a less sensory experience than attending its performance in an audience with others or witnessing it on TV, just as reading a musical score is a far cry from performing it or hearing it performed—though such silent reading does have the aforementioned advantages, for study-purposes, of referability, and pausability/interruptibility.

What about the intermedium, so to speak, of print on a screen: ebooks, Kindle, and the like? A matter of taste, no doubt, and no doubt convenient in some circumstances, but without appeal to this reader. The desktop computer is a splendid tool for research, text-editing, typescript-printing, email, and the electronic PDF-ing of typescript to agent and publisher, but I can't imagine *reading* anything longer than a quite short text on it for pleasure—and even that, if it's a poem or a story, I'd prefer to read on a printed page. While enjoying our print-books on the beach one day, my wife and I borrowed an ebook from a chap at a neighboring umbrella, just to have a look . . . and promptly returned it: thanks, but no thanks! And it was trendy some decades ago to experiment with what was called hypertext: "interactive" e-fiction, the mechanics of which I've happily forgotten. Even such once-amusing structural gimmicks as "books" with unbound, un-numbered, randomly-shuffled pages, or unpaginated "roller-towel" texts whose end rejoined their beginning (an ideal medium, I should think, for such circular texts as James Joyce's *Finnegans Wake*), or pages attached to a spindle so that the "last" page is followed by the "first," seem to have lost whatever piquant appeal they may once have had. Granted that "In the beginning was the [spoken] word," for anything longer than a joke or other than a conversation, a well-delivered reading, or a lecture, give me the *written* word, s.v.p. bindings, numbered pages, *printed* print—long may they live!

THE RELEVANCE OF IRRELEVANCE: WRITING AMERICAN

(Article commissioned by the US State Department in 2002 for inclusion in a book of essays to be distributed in US embassies and consulates throughout the world "to illustrate American values through having various authors consider what makes them an American writer," but subsequently rejected for its "explicit commentary on the events of September 11.")

Speaking at Johns Hopkins University back when his country was riven by apartheid, the eminent South African novelist J. M. Coetzee remarked that under such sorry historical circumstances, for him to publish a novel that made no political statement would be tantamount to his making a very conspicuous—and egregious—political statement. From my seat in the audience I nodded sympathetic assent, although Coetzee's observation was by no means a pitch for sympathy. And, not for the first time, I silently thanked Apollo and all the Muses for affording me the option of political irrelevance.

More exactly, I felt grateful to chance and history for

13

affording me the *option* of writing fiction that intends
no political/ideological statement; for the good fortune
of living in a place and time that can regard as equally
honorable the literary credos of, on the one hand, my
fellow American fictionist Grace Paley, for example—a
heroic protester of US involvement in Viet Nam in the
1960s and '70s, among her other good causes, who once
declared to my students "Art isn't important. *People* are
important; *politics* is important"—and on the other hand
that of the late Vladimir Nabokov, himself a political refugee, who nevertheless maintained that his sole literary aim
was "aesthetic bliss." It should be noted that one can savor a
Grace Paley short story on its literary merits alone (I myself
do not find her excellent fiction especially "political"), and
that Nabokov's virtuoso novels are by no means oblivious
to the political upheavals that drove him from his native
Russia. But both authors felt free—as Coetzee by his own
acknowledgment did not, and as artists in any politically
convulsed or oppressed place and time may well not—either
to engage their art in the service of some political/moral
cause or to regard that art itself as their cause. Art for Art's
sake, or more specifically, in the case of fiction, art for the
sake of language, form, action, character, plot, setting, nar-
ration, and theme: Story (mainly though not exclusively) for
Story's sake. For the freedom to be, in my writing, politically
engaged or politically irrelevant, I feel as fortunate as for the
happy accident of my having been born in just the right
narrow historical "window" (the year was 1930) to miss all
the US-involved wars of the Terrible Twentieth Century:
not here yet for World War I, in which my father served
and my uncle died; too young for World War II, in which
my older brother served; exempted by student and then

marital/parental deferments from service in Korea, where many of my age-group served; too old to be conscripted for the war in Viet Nam—for which my male children, luckily, missed having their draft-lottery numbers called. May the cycle of good fortune be repeated for my children's children! Would that it could extend to all of the world's children!

Which is not at all to say that I regard every one of those terrible wars as unjustified, any more than (as a citizen of my country and the world) I feel "above" engagement with political/social issues. Not at all. Although I happen to incline to the Skeptical-Pacifist persuasion, had I been born a few years earlier I would no doubt have enlisted patriotically in the 1940s, along with my brother, after Pearl Harbor. I will even grant that if such had been the case, I might very well feel the experience to have been centrally important or at least significant to me as a writer: most artists' work is affected in some measure by major experiences of their youth. But I do not regret having missed that particular category of convulsion. Indeed, Ernest Hemingway is the only American writer I can think of who professed a condescending *pity* for those of his countrymen who happened not to experience the trauma of warfare: I recollect his declaring somewhere or other that World War I was "the defining event of their generation, and they simply missed it." Hemingway, however, was by notorious disposition a *macho* adventure-seeker. If his admirable fiction happened to depend upon that appetite, so be it; the no less admirable fiction of William Faulkner, James Joyce, Thomas Mann, Marcel Proust, Virginia Woolf, Franz Kafka, and F. Scott Fitzgerald—to name only a few of his illustrious peers—did not.

My argument is simply that for an artist to be politically concerned and even politically active as a citizen does not—anyhow *should* not, ideally—mandate politically concerned art. I quite understand J. M. Coetzee's position as aforestated, which in his case has produced writing as commendable on its literary as on its moral/political merits. But I admire at least equally the art of the late great Argentine Jorge Luis Borges, for example, who, though embarrassed and harassed by the Perón regime (at whose hands he was "promoted" from his post in the Buenos Aires municipal library to the rank of chicken-and-rabbit inspector in the public markets), was not moved thereby to write political allegories and anti-*Perónista* fables, as he quite justifiably might have been. Borges admits (in "An Autobiographical Essay") to having danced in the streets of Buenos Aires when Perón was ousted in September 1955, and also to writing a couple of pro-Israel poems at the time of the Arab-Israeli war of 1967; more typically, however, when his fiction addresses contemporary political/historical matters—as in his short story "The Secret Miracle," for example, about a Czech playwright executed by the Nazis for the crime of being Jewish—the story is at least as much about art and metaphysics as about the Holocaust.

My own muse is often the one with the grin rather than the one with the grimace. One of our recent collaborations, a comic-apocalyptic "Y2K" novel called COMING SOON!!!, coincidentally appeared just a few weeks after the Islamic terrorist attacks on the World Trade Center and the Pentagon, and in subsequent book-tour interviews and public appearances I was more than once asked whether I thought irony, even comedy in general, to be perhaps *inappropriate*, to put it mildly, in the wake of that atrocity and the subsequent national emergency. Less in my own defense than in defense of artistic liberty and therapeutic laughter, I found myself invoking two of my longtime literary navigation-stars, *The Thousand and One Nights* and Boccaccio's *Decameron*. In the former, the King's anger at his wife's adultery turns into murderous misogyny, ruinous to the state as well as lethal to many of its female citizens: after killing his unfaithful wife and her paramour, King Shahryar "marries" a young virgin every night and has her executed the next morning lest she prove unfaithful, and after three bloodthirsty years' worth of such misguided revenge, families with maiden daughters are fleeing the country in droves. To save her homeland, her remaining "sisters," and the King himself from his madness, Scheherazade volunteers herself (she has a Plan), and the 1001 suspenseful nights of her literally marvelous storytelling ensue. The *Decameron* opens with a scarifying description of the Black Death of 1348: the cataclysmic bubonic plague that in only a few years killed a third of Europe's population, just as the influenza pandemic of 1918 would claim millions more victims than the Great War itself—including that aforementioned uncle of mine, who died of it in France while serving with the American Expeditionary Force. Boccaccio's ten young Florentine lords and ladies retreat from the lawless horror of the dying city to their country estates, where they amuse themselves by swapping a hundred stories: one tale per person per day for ten days (fourteen days, actually, but they take Fridays and Saturdays off), until they deem it safe to return to Florence.

The point of my invoking these classics is that in both

distinguished cases, the stories told in horrific, indeed
apocalytic circumstances, so far from directly addressing
those circumstances, are all but programmatically irrelevant to them. Scheherazade may slip in a tale or two about
people unjustly threatened with death who are mercifully
spared (e.g., Nights 1 and 2), but more typically she goes
in for whiz-bang Special Effects like magic lanterns and
bottled genies, along with erotics and even scatology: one
of Goethe's favorite Arabian Nights was #410: "How Abu
Hasan Farted." After Boccaccio's detailed description of
the plague in Florence, his privileged gentry never speak
of it again until their idyll's conclusion: Their tales have
to do with libidinous husbands and wives (and nuns and
friars), narrow escapes, flirtations, witty retorts; not a word
about how their less privileged *paisanos* are dying miser-
ably by the thousands back in town. Indeed, Romantic
Interest grows among several of the taletellers, and when
they return to Florence and part company at the book's
close, it is not to aid the victims (who anyhow could not
be helped, since neither cause nor cure for bubonic plague
was known at the time), but to avoid the appearance of
having fallen into Vice and to go their separate ways, having judged the epidemic to have passed its peak. A proper
Marxist would be appalled, I suppose; even we mere liberal
Democrats may be given pause by such blithely oblivious elitism, and Boccaccio himself repudiated the book
in his elder years—but on moral, not ideological grounds.
His merry, ribald tales, however, along with the schedules,
rules, and agendas that their tellers improvise for ordering
their pleasures, have served as a therapeutic diversion for
the lucky company, even as an *ad hoc* social order until the
larger world recovers. Their very irrelevance to that world's

crisis, like the general irrelevance of Scheherazade's tales to her being in bed with the Guinness World Record Serial Killer, may be said to be their relevance. Centuries after the horror that inspired and frames them, we read them for pleasure still.

Now: as a matter of biographical fact, I happen to be no fan of the present administration in Washington (George "Dubya" Bush), or of US unilateralism in foreign affairs: no anti-ABM or anti-landmine treaties or Kyoto protocols or International Court of Justice for us Yanks, thanks! Drill the Arctic, cut the parkland timber, cancel *Roe v. Wade*, and step on the gas! And while I quite understand the post-9/11 fever of patriotic display (as opposed to unostentatious patriotism) among my countrymen, it makes me uncomfortable, as does my government's ever more lavish military expenditure at whatever sacrifice of other deserving priorities. In my personal political opinion, the charges against Osama Bin Laden and his al-Qaeda terrorists include their having rescued, with their more serious crimes, an insecure and to some of us lamentable American presidency by permitting it to wrap itself in the Stars and Stripes and imply that criticisms of its right-wing heavy-handedness are unpatriotic. One worries that if the terrorists should strike again, some version of our infamous House Un-American Activities Committee of the 1950s could rise from its well-deserved grave and resume its deplorable witch-hunting. Already, one imagines, complaints like these of mine do not go unnoticed by the nation's reinvigorated agencies of domestic surveillance . . .

In the uncertain meanwhile, however, we Americans remain in 2002 among that minority of the world's population blessedly free, both as citizens and as artists, either to strive for political relevance or—in our art especially—to savor the honorable privilege of Irrelevance. Long may that treasured banner wave!

YOU

An interesting and useful concept, the Second Person: one (or ones) other than I/me/we/us, but closer than he/him/she/her/it/they/them. "You" are the person or persons addressed by me/us: intermediary, as it were, between *us* and *them*. In English, curiously, you're spelled the same whether singular or plural and whether nominative or objective case: *you* remain *you* both as subject and as object of a verb (and when subject, you take a plural verb even when your antecedent is singular), whereas *I* become *me* and *we* become *us*, depending. As a narrative viewpoint, "you" may be either of two things: 1) an *objective* second person other than the narrator, in which case you're almost a *faux* third person ("You hauled out of bed and fixed breakfast," etc.—while I slumbered on?), or 2) a *subjective* second person, which is a *faux* first person ("You wake up, trying to recall what you were just dreaming and still a bit dizzy from last night's drinking. You haul out of bed, fix breakfast," etc.). "You" may also be 3) an *indefinite third person*, as in Heraclitus's maxim "You can't step into the same river twice"—a synonym for "one," and not a feasible narrative point of view.

Do I have your attention? What do you think?
Where are you?
And who?

TWO BITS

. . . of restaurant lore picked up from Paul, the friendly bartender at the old Imperial Hotel, near our summer residence in Chestertown, Maryland:

1) *Ketterzen* (accent on second syllable, echoing the French *quatorziene*): a Yiddish-sounding term for the lucky "fourteenth diner" invited to join—free of charge—a group of thirteen in order to un-*verhex* that unlucky number. And

2) "window portion": the extra-large serving sometimes given diners seated at window tables to attract potential customers passing by. According to Paul, during the Great Depression of the 1930s diners seated elsewhere in the restaurant would often request a "window portion" of their order, *s'il vous plaît*.

Bon appétit!

FACTS OF LIFE: THE PYTHON

"As to the general facts of life and death," the professor then declared, "except for the pleasures of love, good food and wine, music, reading, physical exercise, and a few other things, they inspire me with such horror that, like Robert Louis Stevenson, I must consider it to be only some reflex numbness or self-hypnosis that keeps us all from going screaming mad."

He paused; then raised three fingers.

"Three live chickens are put into the python's cage for his dinner. When he swallows the first alive, the others squawk and flap for half a minute. Then they scratch placidly about the cage, clucking and perching even upon the serpent's back to preen their feathers."

Another pause.

"A sensuous afternoon. A handsome evening. A fine meal. A good story. We are diverted, like those chickens. And we may be grateful (to Whom?) for such diversion, but the python does not go away: it is the very ground we stand on. Any questions?"

I raised my hand.

THE AMERICAN CONSUMER CROUCH

A not-uncommon sight in supermarkets and shopping malls: portly elder citizen, usually, but not always female, bent forward at the waist, forearms resting on handle of shopping cart as if it were a walker, prowling the aisles with plump hams thrust out, often in leisure pants, surveying the merchandise and checking her shopping list. I suppress a condescending smile: she's coping, bless her; providing for herself and, perhaps, a less able mate; deciding what they'll eat and procuring it for subsequent preparation.

Here's to you, ma'am: carry on, and *bon appétit!*

THE SIRENS' SONG

(What those temptresses really sang to Odysseus in Book Twelve of Homer's Odyssey)

"Hear us, exhausted voyager! Your son Telemachus, in vain search of his so-long-absent father, has disappeared without a trace. Your once-faithful wife Penelope, weary of weaving and unweaving her web year after year to forestall her many ardent suitors, and in despair over the absence of her husband and son, has cuckolded you with each of those suitors in turn, and finding none of them to be your superior in the arts of fornication (as best she can recall your matrimonial couplings after so long an absence), has ended her dreary life. As for yourself: forewarned of our irresistible seductiveness and the unimaginable pleasures that we offer, you have plugged the ears of your crew and lashed yourself to your vessel's mast to keep yourself from leaping overboard to enjoy us, but have left your own ears unplugged to hear our irresistible song. Now that you've heard it, why toil on homeward? Come frolic with us!"

Replied the wily mariner, "I'll think about it."

And think about it he did, and dreamed and sighed and fretted about it through many a sea-weary night and day thereafter—but kept on sailing homeward.

CHRYSAORA QUINQUECIRRHA

A pentametric salute to the five-tentacled stinging
Chesapeake Bay jellyfish,
commonly called the Sea Nettle

Here's to *Chrysaora Quinquecirrha*!
Who'd have thought he'd ever live to hear a
Name so lilting lovely laid upon some
Pest as ugly as an old used condom?

CAT MAN

Noticed in main concourse of Chicago's O'Hare Airport: squat elderly fellow about five feet tall, apparently a passenger, pulling a wheeled suitcase with one hand and with the other dragging his Siamese cat on a leash. It's on its side, eyes closed, legs and head tucked, sliding along the polished granite as if dead.

Carry-on baggage?

Carry on, sir! . . .

"LIFT UP YOUR HEADS, O YE GATES!"

Life In (and Out of) a Suburban-American Gated Community

The trade journal *Publishers Weekly*, reviewing a recently published short-story series called *The Development*, praised its "nine darkly comic stories set in a gated community on Maryland's Eastern Shore" as "a searing indictment of a certain sociological class in the later stages of life, when the worries of advancing age beset characters who are dealing with or anticipating infirmities, burdensome care-giving, and wrenching losses . . ."

To the first part of that characterization, the author of those stories here nods a duly grateful "Check"—but he respectfully begs to differ with the second. Although the mid- to upscale gated community of "Heron Bay Estates," in which those "nine darkly comic stories" are set, is purely my invention (to the best of my knowledge, there are as yet no such communities at all on "our" side of Chesapeake Bay, of the sort so popular in other, more heavily developed US venues), I happen to have experience elsewhere of Life Within the Gates, and would call my fictionalizing of it in *The Development* more a Prevailingly Sympathetic Rendition than a Searing Indictment.

My wife and I—contentedly retired academics both, one of whom still spins out fiction that the other indispensably critiques and edits—are fortunate enough to have been able, in our incremental retirement, to dwell for the warmer half of each year in a small rural semi-"development" along a broad tidal creek on Maryland's aforementioned Eastern Shore (which happens to be my native turf, or bog) and then spend the chillier half in—yup—a large but quite pleasant *gated community* on the ever more crowded Gulf Coast of southwest Florida. Two unpretentious, quite different but comparably agreeable living situations, each with its pluses and minuses; we would be loath to trade either for the other full-time, and feel blessed to be able (at least for a while yet) to swap them seasonally like many another American "snowbird," as we Up-Northers are called Down There.

Those pluses and minuses? Our Maryland locale, while gateless, is in fact a "development," more or less: a hundred-plus flat acres of woods and feed-corn fields converted half a century ago into a one-street creekside stretch of two dozen modest houses, most with piers and boats out front, not far from the old colonial customs port of Chestertown. No McMansions, condos, golf courses, clubs, or community pools in the neighborhood, and certainly no gates, security patrols, and such; just the goose-blind and crab-pot-lined tidal creek, the string of comfortably separated houses with their shrubbery and full-growth trees, and behind us several still-farmed acres of corn and soybeans, some vine-clogged hardwood stands beloved by Virginia white-tail deer, and a few marshy ponds frequented by herons and other wild waterfowl. Indeed, we're only marginally a community at all—and we like it that way. Many of us are what native Tidewaterfolk call "C'meres" (people who "come here" to live only part-time, whether seasonally or on weekends and vacations, while maintaining other residences up in Pennsylvania or New Jersey, over in the Baltimore/D.C. area, or down in Florida); the rest are year-'rounders, some of whom have dwelt here from the settlement's beginning. We-all inter-visit a bit, but more often just wave to one another as our cars and pick-up trucks pass en route to or from Town (I'll get to that), or pause for a neighborly chat if one of us happens to be doing yard-work when another jogs, bicycles, or dog-walks by. There's a minimal Property Owners Association with minimal dues, a lightly-used community pier for those whose houses are on the inland side of the road, an annual end-of-summer neighborhood picnic down by that pier—and that's about it. Out-of-town visitors are frequent—friends, grown-up offspring, and *their* offspring—but one sees few resident kids or young adults, not because they're *verboten*, as in some (usually gated) Adult Communities, but because they're busy earning a living elsewhere, whereas most of us, both Up Here and Down There, are retirees. (But not all: thanks to the internet, ex-white-collar types can often go on working in comfortable—and portable—home offices, as do I.) A ten-minute drive through more grain fields and pasture-land fetches us to the attractive 300-year-old riverfront town (population about 5,000), with its Historic District, its good small liberal arts college dating from George Washington's presidency and named after him with his permission (G.W. passed through Chestertown several times en route between Mount Vernon and Philadelphia), a few restaurants, and a few small shopping areas. Couple of hours' drive to the nearest large cities and airports: Washington and Baltimore in one direction, where I can still touch base with the university of which I'm both an alumnus and an ex-prof; Philadelphia in the other, where my wife was born and we were wed.

All in all, "Right nice," as we Eastern Shorers say, and we've enjoyed it for thirty years.

So what's not to like? Not much! What served as our weekend-and-vacation retreat when we were urbanites on the academic calendar became our Main House when we both more or less retired a dozen years ago, and it remains so, although just barely. Much as we miss our long-time colleagues and lively students (a pang eased somewhat by that nearby college) and the amenities of city life, for which we haul periodically back to Baltimore, we do not tire of our country place's quiet and privacy (good neighbors nearby, but no swimsuits necessary either in pool or creek unless there are guests present or crabbers working their trotlines *very* close to shore) and the long, unspoiled water-view out front, where broad Langford Creek ebbs and flows into the broader Chester River, thence into the Chesapeake, the Atlantic, and Earth's adjoining oceans (the first three of those waterways we sailboat-cruised for decades; in our Seniority we're content to explore by kayak their long, shallow, winding upstream stretches). Theaters? Art museums? Concerts? Night life? Not much our cup of tea these days, and anyhow we do occasional traveling beyond those Baltimore/Washington errands—including, in late October and early April, our "snowbird" migrations to and from . . .

A bona fide, unequivocally Gated Community along Florida's Tamiami Trail, which runs along the Gator State's bustling southwest coast from Tampa down to Naples before crossing the Everglades eastward to Miami. Unlike our minimally developed Tidewater Maryland digs, our winter haven is a Development indeed: not a hundred, but several thousand acres near the small city of Bonita Springs (pop. 40,000) a few miles off Interstate 75, which locals like to say drains Midwest Republicans seasonally down to the Gulf Coast the way I-95 drains Northeastern Democrats down to Miami and environs—with numerous exceptions on each side. Having passed along the walls and landscaped berms that screen the "Trail" side of our development, one clears its North or South entrance either by checking in at the appropriate gatehouse, if one is a visitor, or by automatically triggering the gate-lifting bar-code scanner with the decal on one's car window if a resident. The gates lift; their smiling keeper waves from gate-house door or surveillance-camera monitor; WELCOME HOME, bids a sign in the handsomely planted entrance drive, past which one enters a subtropically landscaped, "ecologically sensitive" community of some 6,000 mostly seasonal residents dwelling full- or part-time in the development's five-dozen separately named "neighborhoods" ranging from modest low- and mid-rise condominiums, through "coach homes" (over-and-under duplexes) and more expensive "villas" (side-by-side look-alikes), to detached-house communities—themselves ranging from attractive but unassuming upper-midscale stucco items like ours and most of our neighbors' to multimillion-dollar *palazzi*—and high-rise condo towers. There's an on-site "country club" with three 18-hole golf courses, tennis courts, fitness center, dining and meeting rooms, and other amenities; also a riverside marina club with piers, boat storage, and a members-only restaurant. There are three creekside parks with borrowable canoes and kayaks; "public" tennis courts for us non-club types; periodic concerts and other community events; miles of biking and jogging paths among those several neighborhoods and the numerous lakes, ponds, and "preserve" areas; free hourly shuttle-bus service to the development's well-amenitied beach facility on the nearby Gulf; a Community Activities Center that offers courses ranging from Spanish and French to Living Will Preparation, and meeting-space for a variety of groups: bridge and mahjong, book-of-the-month, Republican Women . . . plus a community website, TV info-channel, and handsomely turned-out periodical newsletter. In addition to the overall Community Association and offices responsible for grounds and landscape maintenance, security patrols, hefty assessment-fee collection, and Design Review of proposed house-construction or renovation, there are less formal individual-neighborhood associations to organize Welcome Back and holiday socials, progressive dinners, and the like.

In sum, a thoroughly developed development indeed. Whether that strikes one as a turn-on or a turn-off depends of course on where one happens to be coming from, literally and figuratively. Having lived and worked for most of our adult lives in chillier northern latitudes—central Pennsylvania, Buffalo, Boston, and even sometimes-ice-slicked Baltimore—like thousands of our fellow US and Canadian Snowbirds we welcome the warm winters, while rolling our eyes at what we call the Florida State Bird (the ubiquitous construction crane) and State Song (the so-frequent wail of EMS sirens en route to vehicle accidents on the Tamiami Trail and I-75, seasonally crowded with us oldsters). Being a couple of standard-issue liberal Democrats, and socially retiring as well as academically retired, we wondered briefly whether we had maybe chosen the state's wrong coast—but the other one is even *more* crowded, and once inside those gates things are tranquil indeed: as quiet and private as our creekside place Back North. Moreover, we lucked into immediate good neighbors with political and other sentiments akin to ours, who introduced us to a few like-minded others, and so at least we're not a minority of two. Good new shops and eateries are added every season to our list of nearby favorites, and the closest air terminal is a mere half hour instead of two hours away. We shake our heads at the area's exponential growth over our decade's residency, not only outside our gates but even within them, where although our "older" residential neighborhoods are all "built out," several new high-rise, high-end condominiums remain under construction despite the nationwide housing slump. It makes us smile that in that little colonial-era township near our Maryland digs, an "older house" dates from George Washington's administration, while one like ours Down Here dates from Ronald Reagan's second term—and is already a likely candidate for renovation or "tear-down." The local newspaper, while more conservative than our Baltimore *Sun* and Washington *Post*, has managed so far to resist the sad downsizing that afflicts many urban dailies as more and more readers get their news online. We sort of miss having a college campus nearby, though there's a branch of the state university up near that airport and (for better or worse) no shortage of college students on the local beaches at Christmas and Spring Break time. The warm dry-season "winter" weather is of course delightful (the wet subtropical summers are another story, but we're not there then, and anyhow Maryland's, while less consistently rainy, aren't much milder). And we get to worry on both fronts through the ever-busier Atlantic hurricane season, not wishing ill luck to others, but hoping that each successive tempest will spare first our stretch of Gulf Coast and then our equally low-lying Chesapeake estuarine system (both our gated and our gateless dwelling-places are officially in Flood Zones, but have thus far been spared serious storm damage, though not several close calls). And like our mainly-conservative neighbors Back North, those I-75 Midwest Republicans in their Lexuses, Mercedeses, and upscale SUVs turn out to be Right Nice folks—so into charitable giving and doing, for example, that the development's annual United Fund drive quickly surpasses its goal, and there are so many volunteers for such programs as English-tutoring for the town's mostly-Hispanic immigrants beyond the gates that my wife practically had to be wait-listed for a shot at it.

Beyond the gates—there's the rub, of course: the exclusionary "Us/Them" aspect of such otherwise so pleasant communities, uncomfortable for folks like us and symbolized several times daily by our ins-and-outs through those automated but 24/7- monitored lift-gates. Granted, in that bustling semi-urban surround there is some comfort in the added security of gates and neighborhood patrols; in having *our* bike-paths, mini-parks, and beach access, and no workers or other non-residents about who haven't been cleared through "Customs," especially since we and most of our neighbors are absent for half the year. But still . . .

So minor and privileged a discomfort is easily lived with,

however, the more so for its being triply temporary: Come spring, we're off with the other Snowbirds—in our case, to that gateless, equally but differently pleasant little Eastern Shore settlement. Come later this century, both venues will most likely be submerged by global warming's rising sea levels. And well before then, some seasons down the road, we thus-far-lucky Golden Agers, like several of our neighbors already both Here and There, will be fetched by disability or death to the end of our migrations.

In the all-too-brief meanwhile, as Psalm 24 commands, "Lift up your heads, O ye gates!" Here come (and go) the "C'meres"!

HARLEY GUY

Seated at a computer in our county library: a ruddy, portly, middle-aged biker type wearing blue jeans, sandals, and green T-shirt with Harley-Davidson logo on the front, and on the back: *IF YOU CAN READ THIS, THE BITCH FELL OFF*. Partly bald head, stringy gray beard and ponytail, paunch so fat that his wide leather belt goes down at a forty-five degree angle from his back to pass under and support his great belly. Parked outside is his big canary-yellow motorcycle with large black leather seats.

I'm mildly curious about what he's looking up on that computer, but am not about to ask.

WEEKLY SPECIALS!

Some while ago, my wife and I stopped at a local garden center to buy some pansies—"on special," as the sign advertised, along with urging us to *Dig In! Plant Now!* A bit later in our shopping expedition she noticed another large sign in the display yard of a tombstone retailer: *Weekly Specials!* Duly amused by the juxtaposition, with a grim grin she suggested, "Maybe we can try to hurry up, honey: Dig in? Plant now? Don't want to miss out on a bargain!"

We supposed that grave-markers aren't exactly hot items (despite old Prospero's declaration in *The Tempest* that his "every third thought shall be the grave"), but this advertisement struck us as a bit over-the-top, more appropriate for a supermarket or a Walmart than a tombstonery. What are they selling over there: Breast of chicken? Long underwear? Then we thought, Well, why not? A nice marble headstone could be an interesting lawn ornament—like a little wishing well or wheelbarrow (except we couldn't plant geraniums in it, my wife sighed, remembering the brightly painted one that used to ornament her old family home each summer). Or perhaps a pleasant companion, like a somewhat overgrown "pet rock": we could cozy up, talk to it, make plans for the future together. Why not get to know the friend we'll be spending so much time with down the road? Get comfortable?

We were half-tempted (well, quarter-tempted) to stop in and ask whether the deal could be sweetened a bit: Buy one, get one free, maybe? But then we reminded ourselves that in fact we already *have* gravestones—footstones, anyhow, in the family grave-plot, inscribed with our names and birthdates and awaiting (long may they wait!) their terminal gravure.

Tant pis: Who doesn't love a sale? Some other week, perhaps . . .

DERMATOLOGY

Jesus loves the little children,
All the children of the world.
Red or yellow, black or white,
All are precious in his sight,
For He loves the little children of the world.

So we White Anglo-Saxon kiddies sang in our Methodist-Protestant-Southern Sunday school in Cambridge, on Maryland's Eastern Shore of Chesapeake Bay, back in the then-totally-segregated South of the 1930s. I don't recall our noticing that irony; if we had remarked it, we would probably have been told that Jesus's *loving* all the races and ethnicities doesn't mandate their integration—the old Separate-but-Equal line, despite the obvious inequalities between our town's all-black ward and its all-white other neighborhoods (which had their own differences, economic and otherwise, but much less pronounced). The four skin-colors mentioned in that hymn translate, of course and more or less, into Native-American, Asian, African-American, and Caucasian, ignoring the rest of the spectrum. As it happens, I never met anyone in those first two

categories until college, and my childhood contact with
Black Americans was pretty much limited to my parents'
very pleasant young housecleaner, "Colored Mattie"—thus
designated (not in her hearing) to distinguish her from one
of my aunts with the same first name.*

"Skin-deep" means superficial (ironically, since the epidermis is our body's largest organ); "thin-skinned" means
hypersensitive; to escape "by the skin of your teeth" means
just barely—but what a consequential membrane one's
epidermis can be! Having been raised in a time and place
when/where skin-color so much mattered ("Paleface,"
"High Yellow," "Mulatto," "Darkie"), and having a father
whose nickname was "Whitey" and whose popular
soda-fountain/sandwich/candy store, *Whitey's Candy Land*,
was located on "Race Street," it bemuses me to see fellow
Caucasians spending hours on the beach or in tanning
salons to darken their pale skin as much as possible. "Black
is beautiful!" (unless, perhaps, one is Michael Jackson,
who obviously did not cotton to that rallying cry). I can
still hear the great Louis "Satchmo" Armstrong growling
a line from the blues song "Old Rocking Chair": "Fetch
me some gin, son, / Or I'll tan yo' hide"—which in his
case would have meant lightening it. "Gimme some skin,
my friend," goes the song made popular by Bing Crosby
and the Andrews Sisters way back when: a request/invita-
tion/command that normally means "Let's shake hands on
that," but can also suggest "Let's get naked." The novelist
John Hawkes memorably called the coming-together of
lovers a "dialogue of the skin"—and indeed, much gets
communicated wordlessly in epidermal intimacy.

---

* Years later, in my early professorial days, I visited then-retired Mattie Spry in Cambridge's
still all-black ward, and learned that she had happily managed to send her own children
to college.

My own octogenarian epidermis happens to be Caucasian to a fault—the fault being a proneness to pre-cancerous actinic keratoses and frequent basal-cell and other carcinomas, mainly but not exclusively on my bald scalp, despite my faithfully applying high-SPF sun lotions and always wearing hats outdoors (even a bathing cap when reef-snorkeling, though not when swimming exercise-laps in a pool). In the days before sun-lotions with SPF numbers, we youngsters sometimes overexposed at the beach and consequently "blistered and peeled": disturbing to remember, and surely conducive to those later keratoses and carcinomas, but par for the course back there back then.

Blessed with privacy from neighbors, my wife and I customarily do our daily pool-laps in the raw—"skinny-dipping," our favorite workout, along with bicycling and brisk walking (for which we dress appropriately). When ocean-bathing, Caribbean snorkeling, or swimming off our tidewater pier, we normally wear swimsuits, but I once had the pleasure of crawl-stroking our half-mile-wide Chesapeake estuary *au naturel* when no neighbors were in sight, and quite enjoyed the freedom from clinging wet fabric, even just my minimal Speedo brief. The slip of silky water along one's entire skin: a midsummer-day's dream (happy anagram for *derma*). Why in the world, I wonder, do so many men nowadays favor *knee-length* swim-trunks? The tyranny of fashion, no doubt—but what a drag (literally) while swimming!

Salted by the Atlantic and freshened by the upper reaches of its innumerable rivers and creeks, our brackish Chesapeake tidewater (as I've remarked elsewhere) has an average salinity approximating that of amniotic fluid and human tears. It can therefore be swum in with eyes wide open—though the swimmer can see little beyond his/her outstretched hand. Its density, and thus its buoyancy, is more than a freshwater lake's or pool's, though less than the ocean's. When vacationing in the salty Caribbean we swim, float, and snorkel for long periods with a minimum of effort, and the warm water-temperatures make wet-suits unnecessary except for scuba-diving, which we don't incline to—too much gear, and no sweet feel of head-to-toe water on the skin!

Beauty, as the proverb warns, may be only skin-deep—but that doesn't make it less beautiful.

Agreed? Then *Gimme some skin, my friend!*

ONLY *ONLY*: THE WANDERING MODIFIER

(in honor of Smokey the Bear's seventieth birthday, August 2014)

Inasmuch as "only" can be either an adjective or an adverb, consider the different meanings of its migration through Smokey the Bear's standard warning to walkers-in-the-woods: "Only you can prevent forest fires."

1) *Only you can prevent forest fires.*
2) *You only can prevent forest fires.*
3) *You can only prevent forest fires.*
4) *You can prevent only forest fires.*
5) *You can prevent forest fires only.*

The first and second declare that no one except you can prevent forest fires: not literally true, but we get the idea, and will be careful. The fourth and fifth assert that forest fires are the only thing preventable by you: not the case either, fortunately—due precautions can often prevent mosquito bites, flu infection, and sundry other bad stuff. The third declares that while you may *prevent* forest fires, you can't do anything about them once they're started: pretty much true—so campers, take care!

Now try floating it through the title of the popular love ballad, "I Only Have Eyes for You" . . .

No other modifier that I know of is so versatile: only *only* (and here it's a noun!).

Happy birthday, Smokey!

JUST A MINUTE

As an adjective, the word *minute* ("myNOOT") means "very small," and indeed, the noun *minute* ("MINnit") is a very small part of an hour. But try holding your breath for a full minute, not to mention putting your finger on a hot burner, and a minute can be an awfully long time. Or consider (but don't hold your breath) how long a minute can be when a misbehaving child is told to "Come here this minute!" In a minute, light can travel 60x180,000 miles (seven laps around the globe), a bullet about seventy-five miles, a car on a highway about one mile, a leisurely bicyclist about a quarter mile, a strolling pedestrian perhaps one-tenth of a mile. The "minutes" of a meeting record its step-by-step (i.e., minute-by-minute) deliberations; a "minuet" is so called because of its small, dainty (minimal, diminutive) dance-steps. And this minute reflection on the several meanings of "minute" should take less than a minute to read.

Every minute counts . . .

DEAD RINGER

A few decades ago, when I was in my fifties and visiting-professoring at Boston University, I happened to see a close-up photograph of myself in a Massachusetts newspaper over the caption *Murder Suspect*. Not me of course, but the fellow (sitting in Plymouth District Court during arraignment on charges that he murdered a thirteen-year-old girl whose body was found buried in the basement of his home) looked so like me that I did a "double-take": same basic features, bald pate, graying hair, short beard and moustache, horn-rimmed eyeglasses, and German surname. My wife and I were utterly struck by the resemblance: I scissored the photo, clipped it to a book-jacket photo of myself taken that same year, and filed it in a folder called *Miscellaneous Material* that I keep on my work-table for possible future reference. I have in fact never referred to it until now, but the fellow's uncanny resemblance to my then self spooks me whenever I leaf through that folder for possible inspiration and come across that clipping: Since he's such a dead ringer for me, is it imaginable that I too could perpetrate so heinous a crime?

Not bloody likely, pardon my adverb, and let's change

the subject: What is a "dead ringer"? Opinion is divided: Google offers one complicated explanation having to do with race-horses and another that I prefer, having to do with the un-dead (I'm writing this in late October, approaching Halloween): in time past, when medical care was even more fallible than today, it sometimes happened that when a coffin was opened for whatever reason, a person thought to have died had in fact been only comatose, and was found not "resting in peace" but contorted by suffocation, sometimes even with garments askew. So widespread was the fear of premature burial that in Victorian England there were several societies for the "Prevention of People Being Buried Alive." Edgar Allan Poe, of course, took advantage of that particular terror ("the most terrific," Poe declared) in one of his most famous horror stories, "The Premature Burial." Indeed, it has been reported that a number of well-known people suffered from this intense fear ("taphophobia"), including, e.g., Frederic Chopin and George Washington. Several biographies mention that while our first president was calm, courageous, and dignified at the end, and while on his deathbed did not seek religious comfort or summon minister or priest, he did request that his body not be buried for at least three days. In fact, the fear of being buried alive was alive and well not only in the eighteenth and nineteenth centuries, but to a greater or lesser extent in all the previous centuries as well as in the twentieth and twenty-first.

To try to prevent such horrors, all sorts of methods were put into play, one of the most often mentioned being a device invented by Mr. George Bateson. According to dozens of reports, lest the "deceased" wake to find himself*

---

* Or *herself*: A European folktale called "Lady with the Ring" tells such a story.

coffined but undead, a string was sometimes attached to his finger and run through a hole in the casket-lid to a bell mounted somewhere or other aboveground, and a night-watchman might even be posted to listen for the bell—the "graveyard shift." "Dead ringer," then, could refer either to the gadget or to the desperate caller (in many accounts the gadget is called "Bateson Revival Device" or "Bateson's Belfry," after its purported inventor). How "dead ringer" came to mean a look-alike, a double, is not definitively explained (but see the Google race-horse business). Nor is it certain that any such device actually existed, since some maintain that much of the above is folklore.

Reviewing these jinglings rings yet another bell: the sad fate of Fortunato in Edgar Poe's "Cask of Amontillado." Dressed as a jester (it's carnival-time), the poor chap is walled up alive in a wine-cellar by Montresor, and the last we hear from him is the jingling of his costume-bells through the wall. The dying ringer? The not-yet-dead ringer? R.I.P., unfortunate Fortunato!

THANKSGIVUKAH

As readers of this may remember, on November 28, 2013, two holidays coincided: the American Thanksgiving Day and the first day of Chanukah, the Jewish "Feast of Lights." Inasmuch as the Hebrew calendar is "lunisolar" and the Christian/secular Gregorian calendar is solar, this was the first such coincidence since 1888, and is calculated to be the last such until some 7,000 years hence.

Our household happens to comprise one "born" Christian and one "born" Jew, both of us essentially "non-observant-secular" since adolescence: technically agnostic—because who knows, finally, for sure?—but spiritually atheist. Given the horrors of human history, including natural disasters such as plagues, floods, droughts, hurricanes, and earthquakes as well as human-made wars and genocides, we subscribe to Voltaire's memorable remark: "God's only excuse is that He doesn't exist." Although we can't get our heads around the idea of an omnipotent, omniscient, and omnibenevolent Almighty who permits, e.g., the Holocaust and other such atrocities, we respect the beliefs of neighbors and colleagues who, whether "observant" Christians/Jews/Muslims/Buddhists/Whatever or not, profess to believe in some sort of God. With a nod to our respective backgrounds, we regularly light a pair of Sabbath candles at Friday dinnertime and the Menorah on the eight nights of Chanukah, and while we no longer bother with a Christmas tree, we enjoy trimming our dining-room chandelier with appropriate ornaments during that season and sending holiday greeting cards to relatives, friends, and former colleagues: an affirmation of ongoing connection, however attenuated, with them, with family history, and with history in general.

So here's to Turkey-Day, and the Feast of Lights! To the English Pilgrims first settling into their New World in the seventeenth century, and to our immigrant grandparents, bless them, making their difficult way here from Europe in the late nineteenth and early twentieth in search of a better life in the Land of the Free and Home of the Brave, and passing that better life down to their descendants. About them we're not at all agnostic: just unreservedly thankful.

DELIVERY

Dear Reader:

Sometimes when posting or opening "snail mail" (actual letters on paper, in envelopes!), it occurs to me that an epistle in an envelope is not unlike a fetus in the womb—folded on itself, awaiting delivery—and that the opening of its envelope by the addressee is a sort of cesarean section (named after the Roman emperor, whom tradition maintains to have been thus delivered: a tradition unsupported by historical evidence). I'm reminded that the snail, in Christian culture, is a symbol of Sloth, one of the Seven Deadly Sins—though there's nothing lazy about sending hand-written letters through the mail instead of . . . *e-pistles*, shall we say?

Etymologically, to *deliver* means to liberate, to set free, as in the Christian prayer "deliver us from evil." In general usage, however, that emancipation is more or less figurative: orators deliver speeches ("addresses," the apt synonym for something delivered); boxers deliver punches; drones deliver missiles; obstetricians deliver babies from the envelope of the womb; and the postal service, UPS, and FedEx deliver packages and mail from sender to recipient.

Speaking of letters: Remember the epistolary novel, that novel-in-letters genre so popular in the eighteenth and early nineteenth centuries (Samuel Richardson's *Pamela* and *Clarissa*, Goethe's *Sorrows of Young Werther*, Mary Shelley's *Frankenstein*, Bram Stoker's *Dracula*)? I perpetrated one myself in the latter twentieth: a behemoth of an offspring called *LETTERS* (seven years in gestation: a lengthy labor!), whose title refers both to epistles and to the alphabetical characters of which epistles and novels are comprised. Letters are the atoms, words the molecules of the written world.

Having delivered myself of these reflections, patient Reader, I've said my say on the subject of Delivery. Best wishes from

Yours Truly

85

On a Fahrenheit thermometer: a very warm day.

On an automobile speedometer: too many miles per hour, except for racecars.

On a birthday cake: too many candles to count—and what mid-octogenarian has enough lung capacity to blow out that many in a single puff?

As I write this sentence (on May 27, 2015), I could give it a try, but my wife and I often no longer bother with birthday cakes or even birthday cards and gifts; we just raise a glass of champagne at happy hour, clink "*L'chaim!*," maybe read a little birthday poem, go out somewhere to dinner, and get on with it—the less fuss the better, with so many birthdays under one's belt.

On with the story?

"Once upon a time . . ."

SYZYGY

In late mornings at my worktable, I sometimes notice that my digital clock reads 11:11—or at other times, that various digital clocks around the house may read 1:11, 2:22, 3:33, 4:44, or 5:55—and I say to myself "Aha: a *syzygy!*"

The term sounds like a Czech or Hungarian surname, but it comes from Greek and means an alignment of orbiting bodies, such as the Sun/Earth/Moon alignments that cause Spring Tides (Some of us may remember the fanciful opening song "The Age of Aquarius" from the "New Age hippie" musical "Hair": "When the moon is in the seventh house / And Jupiter aligns with Mars / Then peace will guide the planets / And love will steer the stars"). And it can apply to other sorts of numerical alignment as well: back in our sailboat-cruising years, for example, my wife and I might notice that our knot-meter was reading 3.3 knots while the depth sounder, just beside it, read 33 feet, and we'd say, "*Voilà!* A syzygy!"

This can be addictive: I confess to an annual minor *frisson* in the late morning of Veterans Day—11:11 on 11/11—and a slightly less minor one at that hour and date in 2011: 11:11 on 11/11/11! It came as no surprise when *Time* magazine reported some years ago that while the number of weddings registered on The Knot website for any Saturday in July is about 12,000, on 07/07/07 the number tripled to 38,000—in part, no doubt, because that luckiest day of the century happened (luckily) to be a Saturday.

Add to the six syzygies in Paragraph One the four three-digit numerical *sequences* that your digital clock displays in any twelve-hour period —1:23, 2:34, 3:45, 4:56—and you have ten noteworthy nothings to watch for in any insomniac twelve-hour period. Now integrate the sequences with the syzygies, and you'll find that they follow each other in regular twelve- and fifty-nine-minute intervals: twelve minutes from syzygy to sequence (e.g., 1:11 to 1:23), then fifty-nine minutes to the next syzygy (e.g., 1:23 to 2:22)—a regular alternation until the show ends at 5:55.

One further peculiarity about them: take any sequence in the series (2:34, for example) and total its digits (2+3+4=9). Now do the same with the syzygy immediately following it (3:33), and you'll find the same result (9). The mysteries of mathematics!

Finally, "Syzygy" also happens to be the shortest English word with three *y*'s, a Scrabble-friend informs me: The three-Y's man? And it contains none of the conventional vowels.

I could go on (and on) about syzygies and other numerical sequences, but won't: it's now 10:11 on 12/13/14 . . .

THE BANALITY OF UNIQUENESS:

A Dialogue

He: Break out the bubbly! Let's celebrate!

She: What are we celebrating?

He: Today's a very special day!

She: It is? What's so special about today?

He: Today is *Saturday, January 31, 2015*!

She: Oh? What's so special about that?

He: Every week there's a Saturday; every year there's a January Thirty-First; every now and then there's a *Saturday January Thirty-First*—but never before in recorded history has there been a Saturday January Thirty-First Twenty-Fifteen, nor will there ever be another! Break out the bubbly!

She: Wait wait wait: Doesn't what you just said apply to yesterday and tomorrow and every other day? Isn't *every* day unique?

He: Absolutely!

She: So their uniqueness is what they have in common?

They're all alike in that every one is unique?

He: The banality of uniqueness! I'll drink to that!

She: Or a unique kind of banality? I'll drink to *that*—unless this conversation has taken the fizz out of our champagne. Anyhow, tomorrow's another day—more or less?

He: So: *carpe diem!*

She: Here's to it!

MISSY:

A Postscript to "The 1001 Nights"

Good evening. My thanks to Professor Khan for his kind introduction; likewise to the University's Department of Near Eastern Studies for sponsoring this lecture series and inviting me to participate in it, and finally to all of you for braving this inclement weather to hear a bit of my story. I wish that this were a peaceful, crescent-mooned evening, but "It was a dark and stormy night" is probably a good way to begin my tale. Shall we?

Okay: as you will have noted in your program, my name is Jamilah-Melissa, which sounds like a hyphenated first name: "Jamilah-Melissa What?" one might ask. But as you may also have noticed, we characters in the *Kitab Alf Laylah Wah Laylah*, or *Book of A Thousand Nights and a Night*, or *The Arabian Nights*, while we may have titles— like "Shah Zaman" or "Sultan Somebody" or "Caliph Whatshisname"—usually go by one name only: my mother Scheherazade, for instance; my Aunt Dunyazade (of whom more to come), et cetera. One of my brothers had two names ("Ali Shar"); the other didn't ("Gharib").

Don't ask me (my name is Jamilah-Melissa).

But now that we've got all hands on deck, so to speak, let me remind you how Mom's story begins and ends. Shahryar, the "King of the Islands of India and China" (whatever *that* means), is so outraged at the discovery of his wife's infidelity, as well as that of his brother Shah Zaman's wife, that he quote "marries" (well, deflowers) a virgin every night and has her killed in the morning, lest she cuckold him. Soon enough all families with maiden daughters are getting the hell out of there, until the country is on the verge of collapse and the Shah's Grand Vizier—whose job it is to come up with a new maidenhead for his boss every night Or Else—has run out of victims.

Whereupon, as you all know, the Vizier's daughter Scheherazade (my mom-to-be) volunteers *herself,* over Grandpa's protests (the Shah had been sparing her as a political courtesy to his second-in-command), asking only that the Shah please let her kid sister Dunyazade (my Aunt Dooney) come sit by the bed to comfort her through her defloration and the presumably final night of her life—not telling him, of course, that their plan is for Kid Sis to then ask whether they mightn't hear a little *story* before all hands fall asleep. The Shah reluctantly agrees to her proposal; groom and bride go to it; Aunt Dooney asks her post-coital question per program; Shahryar gives his OK, and Mom launches into the first of what will be a series of tales-within-tales, timing it to break off in the middle-of-the-middle-of-the-middle-one, more or less and so to speak—right at the crack of dawn, when "the first rooster crows in the east"—and the Shah decides not to kill her until he's heard the end of her story.

Which is to say, her *stories*, since Mom sees to it that whenever one story ends she immediately begins another, to be broken off when the going's good—the narrative equivalent of *coitus interruptus*—on and on for a thousand and one nights. Then, on the thousand-and-second morning, she asks Aunt Dooney to fetch the nursemaids in with her-and-Shahryar's three children, and in they come— "one walking, one crawling, one suckling," so the story goes—and she begs for her life on their behalf: a request that the Shah immediately grants, having long since realized that he loves not only Mom's stories but their teller as well. So he marries Scheherazade; his murderous brother Shah Zaman marries my Aunt Dunyazade; and all hands live more or less happily—not "ever after," but until the Destroyer of Delights rings down the curtain on them and their story.

Now, then: those three kids, of whose serial births and prefatory pregnancies there'd been no mention at all in the course of the thousand and one nights of Mom's ordeal, and of whose gender there is no mention even at the end: the "walker" was my brother Ali Shar, now sixty and living all over the map with his wives and concubines; the "crawler" was my brother Gharib, now a late-fiftyish bachelor, always Mom's favorite because Ali Shar was Dad's; and the "suckler" was Yours Truly—Aunt Doony's favorite, perhaps in part because I was nobody else's until my late, not-especially-lamented husband came along.

Ah, life! And ah, marriages—anyhow the pre-arranged sort. I was still in my teens when they hooked me up with Never-Mind-Whom. Not a *bad* guy, actually; we never really clicked (Hubby was more interested in his work and his assorted concubines than in me), but we got along okay, I suppose, and then *poof!*—the D-of-D saw fit to sink his ship on what was supposed to be a re-enactment of Sindbad's First Voyage. "No sweat," Aunt Doony said: "Your Mom and I will find you another one." But the fact was, I just didn't feel like *marrying* again, perhaps because of my no-better-than-C-Plus first marriage, perhaps because I simply felt no need for it. I experimented briefly with a lesbian connection: not unpleasant, but not my thing. Since then I've been content to be more or less celibate—"Call me *Nun*yazade," maybe?—satisfied with friendships male and female. I don't much miss sex, I guess (well, maybe a little, now and then), but I do miss intimate companionship: a genuine *bond* with somebody, beyond mere friendship and siblingship. Know what I mean?

And that's enough about that. As you may recall, when that *shmendrik* Shahryar (excuse my French) came off his crazy entertain-me-or-die thing and made a proper wife of my mother at the story's end, he then said "Oh, one more thing, Dear: please *re-tell* all those Thousand-and-One-Night stories to my scribes, so they can write them down for our kids and grandkids and the world in general. Okay?" Can you imagine? But Mom, being Mom, said, "Sure, Hon; just give me a year or three." (Do the math: 1,001 divided by 365 equals 2.7424657 or thereabouts.) And by Allah, she *did* it, one way or another: came up with 267 stories (including the tales-within-tales and tales-within-tales-within-tales) plus about ten thousand lines of verse for good measure. Who knows (or cares?) whether the ones that she recited for the scribes are the same ones that she spun out over the years, or new ones that she cooked up as she went along, or some mash-up from the repertory? Mom herself probably didn't know (or care): just get the job done; on with the stories, et cetera! I remember asking her for my usual bedtime story one night when I was a little girl—imagine Mom having to spin out bedtime stories for us kids before going in for sex-and-storytelling, copulation-and-fabulation, with Dad! But she did it, one way or another: that particular night, e.g., when she couldn't come up with a story for me, she said, "Once upon a time, Missy, there was a story that began, quote *Once upon a time there was a story that began* double-quote *Once upon a time there was a story that began* triple-quote *Once upon a time there was a story that began*—et cetera ad infinitum, okay? Or ad nauseam, sweetheart: whichever."

To which I probably replied, "Add *what*, Ma?"

Such a yarn-spinner!

Well: we kids grew up; our parents grew old. Shahryar and Shah Zaman died—*au revoir*, though they were certainly sweeter guys in their old age than they were in their prime—and Mom and Aunt Doony spent their last years together in a nice mid-rise continuing-care condo that we set them up in, on one of the not-yet-overdeveloped "Islands of India and China." More accurately, that *I* set them up in, though my brothers were of considerable help with the moving-in chores after I'd done the searching and finding with Aunt Doony's help.

Dear dear Aunt Doony: What would I have done without her? She was the mother that Mom never managed to be, at least to me; she was the one that I could really talk to, and who would really listen: Mom was too busy cooking up her Entertain-Me-or-Die concoctions, and then repeating them for the scribes per Dad's orders, and then supervising their publication, dealing with agents and publishers and booksellers, not to mention seeing her kids (read "her sons") through adolescence and college, which I would never have managed without my Aunt Doony's help.

Oyoyoy: On with the story?

I mentioned "college": somewhere in my undergraduate adventures I took a course in something like Yarn-Spinning 101, where we actually read Mom's *Thousand and One Nights* and other such tale-cycles, and I learned that a Story involves what's called a "Ground Situation" (or, more technically, a dramaturgically-charged "unstable homeostatic system," like the state of affairs in Shahryar's kingdom before Mom comes to the rescue) and a "Dramatic Vehicle" (enter Scheherazade!), which then Complicates some Conflict through the story's Rising Action to its Climax and Denouement—much like the course of intercourse from titillation through copulation to orgasm and *Ah!* Applying that pattern to my own story-thus-far, it seems to me that what we have on our hands here tonight—or I on mine, anyhow—is a "Ground Situation": Late-legendary-storyteller Scheherazade's middle-aged daughter, now husbandless as well as childless, manages to get by on the lecture circuit, but is looking for a handle on her life's Next Stage, dot dot dot . . .

Questions? No? "Vehicle," anybody, now that we've established my "Ground Situation"?

No Vehicle? Okay, then: I'll catch a cab—and someday, with Allah's help, maybe find my own vehicle and put myself in the driver's seat.

Thank you and good night.

SELF-EXPLANATORY WAKA

(Another traditional Japanese verse-form, two lines longer than the Haiku)

Five beats in Line One,
Seven beats in the second,
Five beats in the third,
Seven beats in the fourth line,
Seven again in the fifth.

WORRY-WART WAKA

Here I sit and fret,
Waiting for her to come home.
Why is she so late?
Traffic jam? Car accident?
Not likely, but . . . Ah, she's here!

BONUS TIME

A few decades ago, when I was in my late fifties or early sixties, an actuarial questionnaire in *Time* magazine informed me that given my medical history, the death-age of my parents, and other factors, I could (barring accident) expect to die in 2013, at age 83. *Okay*, I remember thinking at the time: twenty-plus years to go! On with the story, and my stories!

That was then. Now, as I write this, it's 2013, and I'm 83: less able both physically and cognitively than I used to be, for sure, yet not only still "perpendicular and taking nourishment" (as Senior Citizens at our winter retreat in Florida like to say) but still able to enjoy pool-swimming, bicycling, hiking, and cruise-ship cruising with my merely seventy-year-old wife in this forty-third year of our much-blessed marriage; still able to migrate seasonally with the other "snowbirds" from Maryland's Eastern Shore down to Florida's Gulf Coast and back (but my Mrs. does all the driving these days, along with most of everything else); still able to play baroque recorder duets with my sister-in-law, do my Royal Canadian Air Force stretching exercises every morning after breakfast, go to my desk for a few hours of note-taking and composition, and then chores, errands, and recreation in the afternoon, reading and television in the evening, followed by a good night's sleep—never, however, without the ever-less-subliminal awareness that this so-fortunate state of affairs can't last much longer. No male family-member that I know of lived to be ninety— and who wants to, unless in good health and spirits with one's beloved partner? I accept, therefore, that I'm at least one-third through my presumably final decade; that any year now (or any month, any week, any day) will bring the stroke/aneurysm/cancer/whatever that rings down the curtain on this life's story.

On balance, a quite gratifying story indeed, though not without its share of rough patches. Successful children, now in their sixties and approaching their own retirement; twenty books published as of this date, most of them still in print in one form or another, and translated into twenty-plus foreign languages; an altogether satisfying academic career (never as *impassioned* a teacher as my wife, but certainly a dedicated one, I much enjoyed my faculty years at Penn State, SUNY Buffalo, and especially Johns Hopkins, my alma mater, from which I retired in 1995); books still arriving in the mail from my former students, whom I used to ask at graduation-time to send me their future publications to reassure me that I hadn't seriously damaged them—but no more *un*published pages ever, s.v.p.! And pleasant residences near the old colonial-Maryland customs port of Chestertown (May through October) with its also-venerable Washington College, named for and officially blessed by our nation's first president in 1789, and in the comparatively new but also pleasant community of Bonita Bay in Florida (November through April).

Each of those venues has its pluses and minuses, as what does not? Small-town Chestertown has more limited shopping, restaurants, and the like, but it's blessed with that handsome old college (of which I'm an honorary Senior Fellow, with email and library privileges) and the lovely Chester River, into which flows our Langford Creek, thence into Chesapeake Bay and the Atlantic Ocean: it pleased us to know, back in our sailboat-cruising years, that while we were content to explore the Chesapeake's many rivers, creeks, and coves, we could theoretically set sail down the Bay from our dock, hang a left at Cape Charles, and head east to Portugal! Bonita Springs, on the Gulf Coast between Fort Myers and Naples, has more shops and restaurants but also more traffic, and though our house there is not on the water, our community's stretch of Gulf-shore beach is a mere ten-minute drive. The Maryland place has less-tropical summers, but genuine winters (though mild compared to Buffalo's, with its sometimes epic "Lake-effect" snow-falls). In Florida we rarely have a winter frost warning and can use our screen-enclosed pool for all but a few weeks at the turn of the year, but the summer season there is truly subtropical, with high temperatures and humidity and almost daily afternoon thundershowers. The Atlantic hurricane season impacts both venues with strong winds, flash flooding, power outages, and tidal surges; occasionally we've had to worry about the same storm twice as it moves from Florida up the Atlantic seaboard, but thus far in our thirty-plus years on Langford Creek and our dozen-plus in Bonita Springs we've been lucky: couple of trees down, dock-boards to be replaced, flood-waters up to but never yet into the Maryland house. We knock on wood, cross fingers, make storm-preparations as necessary, sigh with relief when yet another named tempest spares us serious damage—and remind ourselves once again that we really *must* scale down from two properties to one and either live there year-round and do more traveling while we're able, or live south for nine months of the year and find a good three-month summer rental back north (on the water, with private pool and two work/study/computer areas, if such a place exists, and is affordable, which we doubt).*

Ah, denial! But the clock ticks on; the calendar-pages turn. My eighty-minutes-older twin sister died four years ago (emphysema); my three-year-older brother died three years ago (cranial aneurysm); I'm the last of us siblings still standing, breathing air, writing sentences . . .

So? Should one heed Andrew Marvell's advice "To His Coy Mistress" (*Thus, though we cannot make our sun / Stand still, yet we will make him run*—[by] *tear*[ing] *our plea-sures with rough strife / Through the iron gates of life*)? Nah: too old for the Rough Strife bit—been there, done that. "Since we can't make Old Sol stand still," I suggest to my so-gracefully-aging, without-whom-nothing life-partner, "shall we hit the pool-deck? Catch a few rays? Read a few pages, swim a few laps, then a bit of wine and cheese on the dock at sunset?"

Replies she, "Let's do it!"

Bonus Time for sure.

L'Chaim!

---

* Author's footnote, 2017: When I wrote this little essay in 2013, my wife and I were still "snow-birding" seasonally between Maryland and Florida. When maintaining two prop-erties became too burdensome for us, we had to choose between our beloved Chesapeake Bay and southwest Florida's Gulf Coast, and although much of what we love most was in Maryland, like many another North American senior citizen we chose winter-free Florida for our year-round address—and were subsequently whacked there on 9/10/17 by Hurricane Irma, which spared our house but felled numerous much-prized trees and demolished our pool screen enclosure. *C'est la vie?*

INSPIRATION

While awaiting it (more or less patiently) between projects, I'm moved to reflect upon it: *inspiration*, the Muse's CPR. Happening to be a heterosexual male, I'm pleased to imagine Ms. Muse as a lovely woman—don't want to be "breathed into" by some beefy guy! Genius (or invention), said Thomas Edison, is "one percent inspiration and ninety-nine percent perspiration" (with a lot of more or less heavy *respiration* along the way, he might have added). But that 1% is crucial: the spark that ignites the fire. Without it, our "musings" are just so much gas.

"Sing, O Muse," the old epics begin: the fall of Troy, the wanderings of Odysseus or Aeneas, whatever—and in the oral tradition, this invocation of the Muse required literally taking a breath: breathing in, since speech requires exhalation.

Aspiration, inspiration, inhalation. Perspiration, respiration, irritation. Perpetration, *exhilaration*, exhalation . . .

Expiration?

On with the story!

ROMAN À CLEF

Good morning, everybody! Our subject today is that curious and interesting literary genre called the *roman à clef*, or "novel with a key." I trust that you remember from our previous meetings that a work of fiction is a made-up story pretending to be real; it requires the reader's "willing suspension of disbelief" to participate vicariously in the action. Reading Cervantes's *Don Quixote*, for example (often called "the first modern novel"), we know that the nobly deluded hero and his cynical sidekick Sancho Panza weren't actual people who roamed around La Mancha tilting at windmills, but we set aside that knowledge to enjoy the author's satire on the popular genre of chivalric novels and his moving rendition of life in seventeenth-century Spain. Our pleasure comes from pretending that the story is "real" while knowing all along that it's fiction.

The *roman à clef*, on the contrary, is a true (or more-or-less-true) story pretending to be fiction; it requires its readers' willing suspension of *belief* instead of disbelief, and their imagining the "facts" as fiction instead of vice versa. It's a curious and problematic genre: Narrating actual events in the guise of fiction, the author can stack the deck to his/her liking, deciding which characters will be the good guys and which the villains, which events were innocent or benevolent and which malevolent, which accidental and which planned. Notable examples of the *roman à clef* include Saul Bellow's *Humboldt's Gift*, Joseph Conrad's *Heart of Darkness*, F. Scott Fitzgerald's *Tender Is the Night*, Thomas Mann's *Death in Venice* and *Tonio Kröger*, Eric Maria Remarque's *All Quiet on the Western Front*, Robert Penn Warren's *All the King's Men*, and Thomas Wolfe's *Look Homeward, Angel*. Check them out.

Since most fiction includes some facts, and fictional characters may be inspired by or derived from actual ones, and since non-fictional accounts are frequently more or less embellished for effect, the *roman à clef* may be said to lie somewhere on the spectrum between pure fiction and pure non-fiction. Researching the subject on Wikipedia, I learned among other instructive things that libel lawyers advise their writer-clients who want to slander some actual person in a *roman à clef* to use what's called "The Small Penis Ploy": give the target of your derision, among his other faults and shortcomings, a very small penis, and he's not likely to sue you for libel, unwilling to declare indignantly "That's *me* he's talking about!"

Or, don't write *romans à clef*. *Invent* whatever characters are needed for the story's action, just as you're inventing the action itself. Be a masquerader of fiction as fact, not of fact as fiction.

On with the (made-up) story!

MAYDAY!

On this year's first day of May it occurred to me to wonder how "May Day," which used to be an occasion for celebrating the end of winter and arrival of spring, came to be a nautical and aeronautical distress-call. I therefore duly Googled it, and learned from Wikipedia that in 1923 a British radio-operator overheard a French ship-captain in distress calling "*M'aidez! M'aidez! M'aidez!*"—which to his English ears sounded like "Mayday! Mayday! Mayday!" and worked its way into our vocabulary, largely supplanting the old Morse-code "SOS" (dot-dot-dot dash-dash-dash dot-dot-dot: "Save Our Ship!") as radio transmission and then the internet replaced telegraphy in the twentieth century.

Check out on Wikipedia the code's inventor, Samuel Finley Breese Morse—a talented painter as well as an inventor—and be reminded of the first telegraph-message ever sent, from Washington to Baltimore on May 24, 1844 (another May-day!): *What hath God wrought?*

Nobody sends telegrams these days, but as a kid during World War II I well remember how parents with a son in the military overseas feared the arrival at their door of a Western Union messenger with the War Department telegram beginning *We regret to inform you* . . .

HYPERPROPRIOCEPTION

Proprioception (as we all know, whether we know that we know it or not) is physical self-consciousness, our mind's awareness of our body: where our arms and legs, fingers and toes, tongue, and other parts are at any given moment. Without it we could do little or nothing; it's indispensable.

Sometimes when I find myself unaccountably awake at three in the morning, say—in no discomfort, with nothing in particular on my mind, having slept for four hours already and waiting to drift back into another three or four hours of sleep—I have a heightened awareness of that physical self-awareness, and may even take a sort of leisurely self-inventory: Hello there, left earlobe, right nostril, lower lip, tongue-tip, left shoulder, right elbow, genitalia and rectum, left knee, right ankle, left big toe, *et al*. I thank Zeus for my good physical health and that of my beloved, sweetly-sleeping bed-partner. Eyes closed and anatomical roll call finished, I flex my fingers, twitch my nose, and drift back into Dreamland.

WHAT'S IN A NAME?

A rather dizzying realization: that one's *surname* ("second name," "last name," whatever) has not only a *very* long history—going back through who-knows-how-many generations of one's ancestors—but also, somewhere way back there, an origin and perhaps a meaning.

In some cases, the meaning is obvious—a distant ancestor's line of work, say (Archer, Baker, Carpenter, Carver, Farmer, Fisher, Mason, Packer, Potter, Smith, Taylor), or his parentage (Abramson, Johnson, Stevenson, Williamson)—though nonetheless mysterious: Who was the *original* Abram, John, Steven, William? And why were their daughters also called "-sons" (except in Scandinavia, for example, where one finds names like "Kristin Lavransdotter")? And how many generations back was the original Archer, Baker, Carpenter, etc.? In fact, in ancient and even later times and cultures, people had only one name (Socrates, Plato, Aristotle, Scheherazade, Moses): When and why did two names become the norm?

My own unexciting surname—Barth—comes from *Bart*, the German word for *beard*, but I know nothing of my family's history before the end of the nineteenth century, when my paternal grandparents emigrated from Germany to the USA. How many tens, dozens, *hundreds* of earlier generations bore the same surname, and how and why did some original patriarch happen to acquire his name from the circumstance that he sported chin-whiskers? Didn't every man back then? But neither my father nor my grandfather was bearded, even in the days before safety-razors were invented; they either shaved themselves with straight-razors or went to the local barber ("Shave and a haircut: two bits!"). I'm the first of the family in modern times to be bearded—a short one, since the 1960s, maybe to compensate for my bald scalp. My two sons briefly followed suit back in that *Hair* decade, but soon thereafter returned to clean-shaved-ness, leaving me the only bearded Barth in the family.

So? So nothing, I suppose: After all, as Shakespeare's Juliet asks, "What's in a name?"

Now let's consider not people's *first* names (a.k.a. "given names"), but their *nick*names—a.k.a. *sobriquets*, though the terms are not exactly synonymous: A sobriquet is an affectionate or humorous alternative name, often but not necessarily a variation of the original, such as "Ol' Blue Eyes" for Frank Sinatra, "The Boss" for Bruce Springsteen, "Tricky Dick" for Richard Nixon, "Dubya" for George W. Bush, or even "Turd Blossom," the name given by Dubya to Karl Rove. A nickname is usually either *diminutive* ("Frankie" for Frank, "Janie" for Jane, "Susie" for Susan, "Ronnie" for Ronald) or *abbreviative* ("Al" for Alan or Albert, "Bev" for Beverly, "Don" for Donald, "Herb" for Herbert, "Pat" for Patricia or Patrick, and "Nick" [the ideal nickname] for Nicholas). Sometimes it's *both* ("Freddie" for Frederick, "Lizzie" for Elizabeth), or just *alternative* ("Bill" for William, "Dick" for Richard, "Hank" for Henry, "Jack" for John). And there are other sorts of nicknames (often called "pet names") that we sometimes give to people especially close or dear to us ("Buddy," "Slugger," "Lady Bird," "Blossom," "Bunny").

The etymology of "nickname" is curious: the Middle English *an eke name* ("an other name") gets squeezed into a *nekename* ("another name")—the latter a sobriquet, if not quite a nickname, for the former.

And speaking of sobriquets, how about pen-names, or *noms de plume*: "Lewis Carroll" (Charles L. Dodgson), "George Eliot" (Mary Ann Evans), "O. Henry" (William Sydney Porter), "Voltaire" (François-Marie Arouet), *et al.*? Authors have used them for various reasons: to protect their privacy, to avoid gender discrimination, to avoid libel suits.

And then, of course, all these years after the establishment of surnames around the world (except sometimes in Iceland and a few other cultures, where people may be addressed by a given name only), some people, mostly entertainers, have gone back to using just one name ("Bono," "Cher," "Madonna," "Sting").

Let's stop here, in the nick of time (another nick entirely, meaning "notch" or "critical moment"—but that's another story) . . .

LIBRARY FRIENDS

As of our most recent count, my wife and I are more or less official friends of at least five libraries: 1) the Dorchester County Public Library down in Cambridge, Maryland, where I grew up feasting on the Hardy Boys and Tom Swift novels while my twin sister did the Bobbsey Twins and Nancy Drew mysteries; 2) the Johns Hopkins University's Sheridan Library in Baltimore, where back in my college days I defrayed part of my undergraduate tuition by filing books in the Classics stacks and did a lot of fruitful browsing as I re-shelved the *Arabian Nights*, the great Sanskrit tale-cycles like *The Ocean of Story* and *25 Tales Told by a Vampire*, and the racy Bronze-Age Roman satires—good nourishment for an aspiring storyteller; 3) the library of St. Timothy's School over in Stevenson, MD, where Shelly worked her pedagogical wonders for several decades while I was coaching young writers back at Hopkins; 4) Washington College's Miller Library, which I'm pleased to be an official Friend of for occasional research purposes; and 5) more important to us on a regular basis than all of those others, the Chestertown Branch of the Kent County Library and its wintertime counterpart down in

Lee County, Florida, on which we're heavily dependent for everything from must-read new fiction (we keep a list on our refrigerator door) to guidebooks for our travels here and abroad.

Such attractive, *inviting* places these county libraries are—neither intimidatingly large, like the great university research libraries, nor inadequately small—and their so-obliging staff ready to borrow from somewhere else what they happen not to have on their shelves. To us, our public library is more than just a civilized amenity: it's as indispensable as the grocery and drugstore (and a lot easier on the pocketbook). We gratefully borrow books and DVDs from it, and just as gratefully *donate* books and DVDs to it: publishers often send me advance copies of their new fiction in hopes of an advertising blurb, even though I warn them that my vows to the muse prohibit blurbs except for good first books by my former students, and we happily pass those tomes along to the library. What's more, our own shelves being hopelessly overcrowded, when one of those former students or colleagues publishes a book that we must in good conscience add to our house library, we do a kind of *triage* and take some other worthy item off the shelf to give to the county library, even though we know that its shelves get overcrowded too. "What goes around comes around," as the saying goes, and the reverse is true as well: may the library benefit from its occasional surplus-book sales as we benefit from our surplus-book donations. It's a healthy recirculation. And may it not come to pass (as my distinguished contemporary Philip Roth has gloomily predicted) that given the distractions of television, movies, and the internet, "in 25 years the number of people reading novels will be akin to the number now reading Latin poetry." If that turns out to be the case (along with global warming and other apocalyptic scenarios), Shelly and I will be relieved not to be here. Meanwhile, however, on with the stories and the storybooks, novels and poems and polar bears and glaciers and rain forests, and LONG LIVE THE LIBRARY!

NAVIGATION-STARS

The firmament of literature is ablaze with stars of every magnitude: too many even to count, much less to read. But just as celestial navigators of old chose from that dazzling overabundance certain first-magnitude beacons to steer by, writers of fiction or poetry will have been significantly influenced by particular predecessors, as well as by particular life-events, mentors, gender, ethnicity, sexual orientation, and other circumstances, and will consciously, half-consciously, or unconsciously steer by those stars through their artistic odyssey.

Speaking of which (the *Odyssey*): my own short-list of principal literary navigation-stars begins with Homer's Odysseus, the paragon and prototype of the Mythic Wandering Hero, as famously defined by Joseph Campbell. Homer's epic *Iliad* impressed but never much moved me: those crazy-jealous Olympian deities, the slam-bang warfare, the Trojan Horse gimmick . . . But the post-war *Odyssey*, with its stressed-out veteran's long journey home, his temptations and seductions by Circe and the Sirens and his resourceful dealing with them (plugging his shipmates' ears against the Sirens irresistible calls, e.g., but lashing himself to his ship's mast with ears unplugged in order to hear the Sirens' song but not be seduced thereby), and his equally resourceful wife Penelope's strategy of forestalling her persistent suitors by endlessly unweaving and re-weaving her web—brilliant!

And a hard act to follow, as they say in showbiz. But my second navigation-star (*historically* second, not second in importance: these four are equally important to me) follows closely on Homer by being nothing like him: it's Anonymous's Scheherazade, the heroine of *The Arabian Nights*. Scheherazade's bedtime stories to her homicidally demented royal spouse are certainly entertaining, but her entertain-me-or-die "Ground Situation"—the oral-narrative equivalent to "publish or perish"—is what sets the Nights apart from such other admirable tale-cycles as Boccaccio's *Decameron* and Chaucer's *Canterbury Tales*, with their multiple tale-tellers: they tell their tales to stave off boredom; she tells hers to save her life and her country. I came to know Ms. Scheherazade (and Boccaccio and Chaucer and many another yarn-spinner) as a very green undergraduate student at Johns Hopkins University, helping to defray my tuition expenses by working part-time as a book-filer in the university's "Classics" library and not infrequently borrowing from the return-cart items not present in my course-curriculum: such genre-busting (or at least genre-stretching) marvels as Rabelais's *Gargantua and Pantagruel*, Somadeva's *Ocean of Story*, Sterne's *Tristram Shandy*, Diderot's *Jacques the Fatalist and His Master*, and many another.

Star #3 is less dramatic, but no less richly entertaining: Cervantes's *Don Quixote*. Him too I first met as an undergrad, not this time on the book-return cart but in

a wonderful "Great Books" course in which we studied
each item with a professor whose specialty it was: Dante's
Divine Comedy with Charles Singleton, Thomas Mann's
Magic Mountain with Leo Spitzer (a refugee from Hitler's
Germany), and *DQ* with Pedro Salinas, an elderly poet-ref-
ugee from the Fascist Spain of Generalissimo Francisco
Franco. Splendid mentors all, and I have a particularly
fond memory of reading Cervantes with Salinas *en Español,*
not only because I so enjoyed that book and that professor—I enjoyed them all!—but because of a moment especially felicitous for a callow undergraduate like my then
self, less prepared than my classmates who'd graduated
from good urban high-schools or private schools, unlike
my poor dear rural high-school which back then didn't
even have a twelfth grade. "When is the first moment in
the book," Salinas asked us, "when Don Quixote *acts* on
his mad delusion of knight-errantry?" The consensus of
the class was that it was when Quixote mistakes the windmills for giants, attacks them on horseback with his lance,
and gets knocked to the ground, but seeing Salinas smile
in a certain way, I bethought myself and ventured that it
was much earlier than that: well before he sets out astride
Rocinante with his side-kick Sancho Panza alongside on
his donkey, Quixote, in preparing his armor, improvises a
helmet-visor from paper and tests it with his sword; when
it cuts easily in half, he makes another just like it, but this
time declares it satisfactory and dons it without repeating
the test. Perhaps *that's* the telling moment?

Salinas smiled, then said in effect that in the lengthy
history of commentaries on *Don Quixote,* to his knowledge
only two have remarked on that moment: "Myself, and
now Señor Barth." I'm sure that I must have blushed with

embarrassed pride; even sixty-plus years later, his compliment still tingles in my memory. I like to think that it may have inspired me to imagine that I too might someday become a *writer*, and I know for a fact that it encouraged me as a professor to remark and praise in class analogous insights by my students. *Muchas gracias*, Don Pedro!

My fourth chief literary navigation-star is Mark Twain's *Huckleberry Finn*, the raffish, mischievous, juvenile, and *very* American equivalent of Odysseus and Quixote. Like them, he rambles—not over seas and plains, but down America's central artery, the Mississippi; not on a ship or a horse, but aboard a makeshift raft; and not with Squire Sancho Panza as a sidekick, but the no less memorable Nigger Jim (pardon Twain's adjective). While Huck is not half-crazy like Quixote, not dealing with monsters, gods, and demons like Odysseus, and not yarning to save the show like Scheherazade and Homer's Penelope, he epitomizes adolescent rebelliousness in its American flavor. Twain's *Tom Sawyer* is a fine novel; its sequel is a navigation-star masterpiece.

So. Odysseus, Schcherazade, Quixote, and Huck: the North/East/South/West of my literary compass, with whose aid I steer my own course from project to project. Thank you, *maestros*!

THE LIVES OF OUR STORIES

"The story of your life," it has been remarked (by Yours Truly, in some essay or other), "is not your life; it is your story." And not only do our lives have stories; our stories have lives as well: some are stillborn or short-lived; others are virtually immortal; others yet experience serial lives, multiple simultaneous lives, avatars, reincarnations. Years or even decades after their original publication, one's published stories may resurface in anthologies, translations, adaptations into film or television, and their author may come to feel as estranged from them as from his or her then self. Moreover, the stories themselves change, not only in translation from their original language or medium into others, but likewise in subsequent revisions, and in our perception of them as we and the times move along. "I thought *that* back then? No way!" Or on the other hand, perhaps, "Hey: well said! Don't think I could bring it off that well nowadays . . ." In the American edition of my 1958 novel *The End of the Road*, for example, the cuck-olded husband Joe Morgan complains to his friend Jacob Horner, who has cuckolded him, "Why in the name of Christ did you fuck Rennie?" In an early British edition the line was changed to "Why in the name of Christ did you *bed* Rennie?"—despite the Brits' calling the f-word back in the 1940s "the word that won the war." (Subsequent British editions restored the correct wording.)

Our life-anecdotes, too, have lives and half-lives: our accounts of childhood, adolescence, first love, marriage, vocation, career, retirement, and dotage change over time, as do their tellers. Indeed, the self-styled "neurophilosopher" Daniel C. Dennett, in his treatise *Consciousness Explained*, defines the "self" as "a posited center of narrative gravity"—a center always in motion and flux. Heraclitus's famous observation that you can't step into the same river twice is apt not only because the *river* keeps changing, but because the "you" is ever-evolving (or devolving) as well: "you" are not quite the person that you were five years ago, not to mention twenty or thirty years ago. And what applies to that river applies likewise to "the ocean of story."* The corpus of literature, like the human body, is ever-changing. Things are added, subtracted, lost, found, modified, revised: sometimes slowly, sometimes suddenly; sometimes for better, sometimes for worse. Whole genres die, or virtually die (the epic saga-poem, the sonnet-sequence); some, like the novel and for that matter the whole medium of print-literature, are pronounced dead or at best moribund, yet manage not only to persist but at least occasionally to thrive. Happily, like giant sequoia trees, some literary species are in no hurry to expire; one could write a very long novel about The Death of the Novel.

As I was saying . . .

---

* The original *Kathasaritsagara*—literally "The Ocean of Streams of Story"—is a multi-volume compendium of Sanskrit tales-within-tales (and even tales-within-tales-within-tales) assembled in the eleventh-century by Somadeva. For more on this and other multiple-framed stories, see my essay "The Ocean of Story" in *The Friday Book* (New York: Putnam's, 1984).

"THIS IS NOT A STORY"

In 1929, just when the stock market was about to crash and precipitate the Great Depression, the Belgian Surrealist painter René Magritte produced a large, simple painting of a pipe, under which were the words *Ceci n'est pas une pipe*: "This is not a pipe"—his way of reminding us that a *painting* of a pipe is not an actual, smokeable pipe, any more than a painting or sculpture of a lovely nude woman is an actual, embraceable woman (despite what Pygmalion might say about that). In short, that Art is not (first-order) Reality, though of course a painting is itself a real object—in many cases, much more valuable than its subject. A pipe like the one in Magritte's painting could have been bought from a Parisian tobacconist back in 1929 for a few francs; the painting (now in the Los Angeles County Museum of Art) is probably worth millions of dollars.

Mutatis mutandis, as they used to say in Rome, what you're reading here is not a Story, much as it might aspire to be. A real story traditionally has a Beginning, a Middle, and an Ending: exposition, conflict, complication, rising action, climax, denouement. *This* would-be "story" can't get its ass out of bed, off the ground—whatever a story's ass is supposed to do. Real stories have *characters*; I haven't met any characters hereabouts yet, only a mumbling narrative voice, an anonymous first-person-singular pronoun of unspecified gender, ethnicity, age, and curriculum vitae. Who am "I"? Herman Melville opens his novel *Moby-Dick* with the sentence, "Call me Ishmael." I was tempted to open this whatever-it-is with, "Don't call me; I'll call you (or not)"—but that's no way to get a story going, so what the hell: just call me *Fred*. Better yet, since that's a man's name, maybe call me *Manfred*. Okay?

Okay, okay—who cares? On with the story.

What story? *Real* stories, as has been mentioned, begin with a Beginning, like maybe, "In the beginning was the Exposition . . ."

Nix that: in the beginning was this schmuck "Manfred," scribbling scribbling one sentence after another, hoping (thus far in vain) that something would

CLICK!

Um: Once upon a time there was a story that began (those were the days) *Once upon a time there was a story that began* (*those were the days*) **Once upon a time there was a story** [et cetera ad nauseam] . . .

CLUNK.

Fresh start? "Manfred Zilch, English-speaking male of a certain age and uncertain self, thus-far-unsuccessful scribbler of sentences aspiring to begin a bona fide by-God *story*, attempted once again by writing *Manfred Zilch, English-speaking* (struck-dumb)

CLUCK?

Ahem: On the eastern shore of Maryland's Chesapeake Bay (more specifically, on the western shore of the Delmarva Peninsula, which peninsula includes the state of Delaware, the Eastern Shore of Maryland, and the Eastern Shore of Virginia), there occurred in 1929—along with the aforementioned stock-market crash leading to the Great Depression—the successful expulsion from his mother's womb of Manfred Z____, later known (just barely) as "Manfred Zilch," author of mostly-unpublished "stories" that earnestly *aspired* to be stories but seldom realized that aspiration, their problem being that like the old crank-start automobiles before self-starters were invented (just about the time of MZ's birth), they wouldn't . . . effing . . . *start!*

"Except," declared MZ's ballpoint pen to his notebook, and then his fountain pen to his first-draft looseleaf binder, and then his keyboard to his word processor, the sentence more-or-less-in-progress gaining (or at least striving to gain) momentum before it resumed, as now it must, or anyhow will, "that this one seems to have *started,* no? As of this word (I mean the word *word*), we're 630 words into it; 635 if we include the five immediately following that parenthesis and count '630' as a word; 651 if we include the clause beginning with '635,' et cetera ad infinitum ad nauseam ad whatever end of quote"—and end of much-too-complicated sentence.

Are we having fun yet? Not "Manfred Zilch" (whoever that isn't). *He* wants to write a bona fide *story,* with believable *characters,* palpable *settings,* feelable *conflicts* and *emotions,* not "metafictive" blahblahblah . . .

Like "Once upon a time there was a dark and stormy

night"? Or maybe "Twice upon a place there was a bright calm day"? Or perhaps "Get your shit together and tell us a goddamn *story*, Zilch-o!"

Dum-dee-dum-dum . . .

Dumb-dumber-dumbest!

Dum-dee-*da-da*? No: Dada had its short-lived day back in the Nineteen-Teens—Marcel Duchamp, Francis Picabia, Man Ray, Tristan Tzara, *et al.* Now we're in the *Twenty*-Teens: Dada's Grandchildren, some of us in our last-lap eighties, on Social Security with aesthetic insecurity, but still doggedly (kittishly? mulishly?) endeavoring to *tell an effing story*, dot dot dot, on a hot humid breezeless mid-July morning at our work-table in our workspace in our house/apartment/condominium/whatever in Sometown, Somestate, United States of Anywhere—and managing, against all odds, to have thus far perpetrated three pages of yadayadayada while waiting for our dormant-if-not-deceased Muse to get off her sweet lazy butt and

KNOCK KNOCK!

Who's there?

NOBODY

Nobody who?

Nobody in her/his right mind will put up with this meta-crap much longer, so let's give it one last try:

"What *I* think," here interposed MZ's partner "Sally Forth" (her name in quotes because while it is in fact her real name, she being the daughter [and fourth child!] of the late Harold and Elizabeth Forth of Baltimore, MD, USA, the accidental wordplay makes her wince; yet like many of her "Women's Lib" generation, despite her being legally married to "Manfred Zilch" she maintains her maiden surname [she also winces—as who wouldn't?—at her spouse's surname]), "is . . . I forget what . . ." But then she remembers: "Oh, yeah: I think we should hit *Restart*."

"Restart?" wonders her writer's-blocked author-husband. "Like back to 'Once upon a time'? Or maybe 'The Subject verbed the Object'?"

"No no no. How about 'When Manny first verbed Sally'?"

"*Verbed*? Would that be 'Saw'? 'Met'? 'Touched'? 'Kissed'? 'Groped'? 'Et cetera'd'?"

"And here we are: take it from there, Love: *one. Two* . . ."

"And three's a crowd, so it's just us two, and *there* is here, and *here* is now, so it's Manny and Sally in the sentence-in-progress on page whatever of this wannabe story bumbling in the Muse's womb—"

"Or rumbling in the Muse's gut like a fart-in-the-works . . ."

"As you wish, Ma'am—bearing in mind that a fart-in-the-works may be the digestion of a memorable repast, just as a story-in-the-works may be the digestion and transmutation of a memorable experience."

"E.g.?"

"*Exempli gratia*, the day when Manny first met Sally, and vice versa. It wasn't *he*, by the way, who verbed *her*: my happy memory is that they first tentatively and then enthusiastically verbed *each other* in the king- or queen-size bed in the motel near the college where he'd given a reading earlier that evening which she'd attended—she being an admiring fellow academic at another branch campus of the same state university who had met him a few times at various academic occasions and exchanged ever-more-friendly letters with him from time to time, and they happening both just then to be putting a regretfully failed first marriage behind them, dot dot dot . . ."

"Dot dot dot indeed: that night we dotted our eyes, crossed our t's, hugged and kissed, talked-talked-talked, and verbed our butts off till the crack of dawn. Did we sleep at all?"

"Who knows? We were young then—anyhow a lot younger than now—and just starting Our Story: not Hers and His, but *Ours*."

"*Vive notre* story! On with it?"

"*Comme il faut*, pardon my French."

"Ah, that day! That first night!"

"Two-score years ago, give or take a few months: our Book of Fourteen Thousand Six Hundred Nights."

"Since which first night we have eaten . . . let's see . . . [*punches pocket calculator*] . . . forty-three thousand eight hundred meals? Cuddled and slept together all but a few of those fourteen-thousand-plus nights, engendered zero offspring, but taught thousands of students and scribbled thousands of sentences, even *publishing* a few pages of them here and there."

"And here we are, dot dot dot."

"Enough with the dots. On with our story?"

"Or non-story, whatever. The tellable part of it now more or less told, the rest nobody's business, except ours."

"Because—as has somewhere been said by somebody or other—*the story of your life is not your life; it is your story.*"

"*One* of our stories. Happy ones. Sad ones. X-rated, PG—the whole whatever-the-Yiddish-word-is . . ."

"*Megillah*?"

"The whole Scotch-Jewish McGillah."

"On with it?"

"On with *them*: once, twice, thrice upon a time . . ."

"If the joint SallyManny memory is correct, they have in fact coupled/copulated as much as thrice-upon-a-night in their younger, more ardent and vigorous years—not often, but surely once or twice or thrice. Those were the nights!"

"And these are these: let's say 14,600 and counting: 14,601, 14,602 . . ."

"Yawn. Climax, *s'il vous plaît*? *Denouement*, pardon my French? French kiss, maybe?"

"*Genug*, as we say *auf Deutsch*. *Basta*. *Sufficiente*. Enough already! You call this a *story*?"

"No, *nein, nyet, et cet.*"

THIS IS NOT A STORY.

REMEMBERING BILL

Eulogy for William Herman Barth:
04/26/1927–01/06/2010

My brother, Herman William Barth III, was given his first
and middle names in memory of an uncle whom we kids
never got to meet: our dad's older brother, a young sculp-
tor who served in France with the American Expeditionary
Force in World War I and died there in the great influenza pandemic of 1918. "Uncle Herman" had been
named in turn after our grandfather, Herman *Wilhelm*
Barth, a German immigrant stonecutter who'd established
a tombstone-carving business in Cambridge, Maryland.
Our granddad Englished *Herman Wilhelm* into *Herman
William* when naming his son, and then my brother later
Englished *his* name further by switching *Herman William*
into *William Herman*. But to us he was always "Bill," and
of the many qualities that his kid brother admired about
the guy, I'll speak here of four: his energy, his adventur-
ousness, his multiple enthusiasms, and his resilience in the
face of setbacks.

    When we-all were growing up in East Cambridge

during the years of the Great Depression and the Second
World War, Dorchester was the only county in Maryland
that couldn't afford a twelve-year public school system.
The few better-off kids in town were sent to private schools
for their junior and senior years; the rest of us graduated
from eleventh grade at age seventeen. But Bill was such a
bright and energetic student that he skipped fifth grade,
graduated from Cambridge High at the even more tender
age of sixteen, and scored a scholarship to Johns Hopkins
University—the first in our family ever to "go off to college," as they say, except for Uncle Herman, who had studied sculpture at the Maryland Institute of Art before going
off to fight his father's Fatherland. But young Bill found
the rigorous engineering curriculum that he'd signed up
for at Hopkins not to his liking, and chose to leave after
one semester.

A disappointment, no doubt, to all hands; Bill's
ever-upbeat reaction, however, was to sign on promptly
aboard a US Coast & Geodetic survey vessel (World War
II was in horrific full swing by then, but he wasn't even
draft-age yet) and spend the next year happily taking nau-
tical-chart soundings from Chesapeake Bay all the way
up-coast to Maine and back down to Norfolk, Virginia.
There he bought himself a jim-dandy Cushman motor
scooter, drove it home to Cambridge, and, having turned
seventeen, handed it over to me "for the duration" and
enlisted in the Army in time to reach Germany with our
occupation forces just after V-E Day. By his eighteenth
birthday, Sergeant Bill was featured in the Army's *Stars
& Stripes* newspaper as the youngest non-commissioned
officer in the European Theater of Operations. Myself
being a green fifteen at the time, too young for military

service, I sort of envied him all that. When Sergeant Bill was mustered out, he brought his kid brother a fine souvenir Omega wristwatch that served me faithfully for the next thirty-five years, until it drowned while snorkeling off a cruising sailboat in the Virgin Islands and was buried at sea off St. John. I still miss it.

Ex-G.I. Bill then returned to college, at Salisbury State with the help of that *other* G.I. Bill, and this time around did well indeed, scoring high grades and an Eastern Shore girlfriend, Martha Jane White, whom he would subsequently marry and sire a fine family with—a family that it has always been a pleasure for Shelly and me to feel ourselves part of. Somewhere along there too he chose a profession, went from SSC to University of Maryland Law School, and spent some busy next decades in the D.C. area as a husband, father, friend, and government lawyer, first with the Army's Quartermaster Corps, then with the General Accounting Office.

It being characteristic of Brother Bill to do a thing well, enjoy it thoroughly, and then move on to some New Next Thing, in mid-life he remarried, retired at age fifty-four from his profession (which, *un*characteristically, he had never greatly enjoyed), and with his new bride moved clear across country to northwest Washington state to pursue a whole new spectrum of hobbies and interests that I never knew the guy had. Out there in Sequim he helped build his own house (designed by one of his new stepsons) and lost a fingertip in the process. Among many other pleasures, he worked in stained glass, became a formidable chef who smoked his own salmon in several different kinds of smokers, made his own wines and beers, and whipped up hundreds of hors d'oeuvres and dinners for friends and guests. He trained to be a white-water rafting guide (just for the sport of it, with no intention of doing it professionally) and became a tireless and adventurous traveler as well, often preferring to stay with local host families even if it meant in cramped and meager circumstances. He and Dorothy went literally around the world (and seemed to remember every detail of everything they saw and the people they met; what stories they had!): across the wilds of Siberia, up the rivers of China, above the Arctic Circle, and down to Antarctica, bringing Shelly and me such souvenirs as a handsome ulu-knife from Inuit-land, a menacing Mexican demon-figure called Tlocolorero, and a wood-carved rabbinical-looking statuette whom we named "Shmuel," picked up in some Eastern European former ghetto. That couple (I mean Bill & Dorothy, not Tlocolorero & Shmuel) thought nothing of hopping into their Toyota Prius and driving from Washington state cross-country to Maryland, then down to Florida, over to Louisiana for some Creole cookery, out to California, and back home to Sequim, visiting their many friends and relatives as they circumnavigated the USA, sometimes tent-camping in the snowy national parks. Even in the closing chapter of their life together, as Dorothy's unfortunate cognitive condition worsened, to our amazement they managed a boat-trip down the Rhine, revisiting the country that Bill had helped to occupy sixty years before and from which our grandfather had emigrated in the 1880s. Shelly and I have done a fair amount of world traveling ourselves, but by comparison we feel like stay-at-homes! And it's typical of Bill's resilience that after coping with Dorothy's terminality and death, with a lot of help from his family he was able to put behind him the house and life they'd built together and shift cross-country one more time to commence what we all hoped would be a gratifying Last Chapter Back East with us. It was, alas, much too short a chapter.

One final story and I'm done. Among my brother's innumerable skills and hobbies was a facility with knots and knotting that I suppose he picked up in his Coast & Geodetic Survey voyaging. Both Shelly and I (and, we suspect, dozens of other family-members and friends) still have nylon macramé belts that Bill braided for us somewhere along his way. Our favorite Bill-braid, however, was what's called a Turk's Head: an intricately woven white nylon band on the upper rim and "king spoke" of our cruising sailboat's steering wheel, which he spent several *very* sweaty summer hours braiding for us back in the mid-1980s so that whoever was at the helm would know when the vessel's rudder was aimed straight ahead. For two-dozen Chesapeake-cruising years, Shelly and I steered our course with the aid of Bill's Turk's Head: a fitting reminder of big-brotherly beneficence, at which we often smiled our gratitude.

As we do here again: Many thanks, brother-of-mine— and *bon voyage*.

I'LL SEE YOU IN MY DREAMS

As I approach my eighty-eighth birthday—in good health and good spirits, in the forty-eighth year of happy marriage to my beloved Shelly—it occurs to me that either I almost never have dreams these days or almost never remember them. Is that perhaps because they've all more or less come true? Or is it because, as another old song declares, "Life is but a dream"*? The most likely reason is that my memory has become unreliable. Whatever the case, back in the day I believe that I recalled my dreams about as often as most people do, and several decades ago I woke up remembering one so vividly (and disturbingly) that I took the trouble to write it down. Now, thirty-eight years later, I've happened to re-find and reread that transcript, which, bemused, I here pass along: make of it what you will . . .

Shelly and I are stopping in, or are wandering through, a strange semi-residential hotel: labyrinthine, seedy, ramshackle, once elegant but badly run down. Now I'm

---

* "Row, row, row your boat, / Gently down the stream. / Merrily merrily merrily merrily, / Life is but a dream." The title song, *I'll See You in my Dreams*, is by Isham Jones, 1924.

looking for her from hall to hall, up and down strange Escher-like stairways and additions. I've lost track of her!

As I wander through the place, I sip from a tiny glass of beer, the size of a shot glass, and am disgusted to find a drowned insect on my tongue and two more in the glass: insects on the order of lake flies. I spit it out and remove its companions from the beer with my finger. Then, despite my disgust, I sip again, and am appalled to find not one but several more bugs in my mouth and even more in the glass! I dispose of the glass, which must be attracting them, and now in vigorous disgust finger the dead insects from my mouth. Even as I do, I realize with horror that they are not getting into my mouth from the glass, but vice versa: my mouth is filled with dead insects; they are multiplying there! I spit and pull out clumps of them, frantically, and still feel others inside.

This passes; I reach a small lobby. A woman whom I vaguely know and who apparently works at the establishment (a combination beauty parlor and women's steam bath) sympathetically informs me that my wife is in the steam room, no longer capable of recognizing people she knows. The woman goes to fetch her for me; she enters the steam room and closes the door; is gone a long while. Finally I open the door: in the steam are many women, either naked or in hospital gowns. The vaguely familiar woman is naked, evidently her working costume; with unembarrassed dignity she wheels Shelly out in a wheelchair of sorts. Shelly wears a wrapper and shower cap, and doesn't recognize me. In great distress I wheel her through the lobby, out of the hotel, through difficult glass doors and around tight corners, into some sort of subway station. As we wait for our train, groups of Hell's Angel types (but more colorful than menacing) are mounting long "tandem" motorcycles, each oddly with half a dozen seats in a row.

We take our train, and now Shelly is missing again, and I'm searching everywhere for her. The train comes in for a landing like an airplane, in Boston; overshoots its normal stop and deposits me on a high-security military pier in the Navy Yard, where odd-looking drone aircraft and missiles are kept. My violation of security causes no problems. It is beginning to rain, and night is falling; I step inside a building and meet a Navy chap who turns out to be my wife's old boyfriend from their high-school days: Larry Kupferberg. He informs me, sadly, that Shelly has turned up there, still *non compos mentis*. A terrific night-firing exercise begins, in blinding rain; through the plate-glass windows of the office we watch green fire-bursts in the torrential night sky, while I wonder what to do now.

I wake, with the feeling of having lived in a strange novel, and am much relieved (though not surprised) to see that my beloved is sleeping peacefully beside me . . .

Have fun, Freudians!

SOME REFLECTIONS ON
SCOTT FITZGERALD

(Originally delivered at the F. Scott Fitzgerald Conference in Baltimore in October 2009, subsequently mislaid in my files, recently re-found, and here redelivered.)

My job-description this evening is to read a couple of favorite passages from the writer whom we're here to honor and then to speak informally for a few minutes about those passages and their author. Assuming your permission, I'll do that in reverse order.

It's embarrassing to report, in this company, that in fact I don't *have* any particular "favorite passages" from Scott Fitzgerald's *oeuvre*—or anyhow *hadn't* had until quite recently. I'd read and enjoyed a number of his novels and stories back in college days, but their author had never been among my literary models, like Scheherazade, James Joyce, and William Faulkner during my apprenticeship, or Jorge Luis Borges in my mid-career (my 1968 short-story series, *Lost in the Funhouse*, was inspired by my discovery of Borges's *Fictions*, and when I happened to mention that circumstance to Italo Calvino during his visit to Johns Hopkins, he told me that his *Cosmicomics* were likewise his attempt to assimilate Borges). My wife, Shelly, who sometimes taught *The Great Gatsby* to her high-school students, could, I'm sure, quote any number of Favorite Passages from that novel and from Fitzgerald's stories. But a dozen years ago, when I accepted with grateful pleasure this organization's Scott Fitzgerald Award, the only Fitzgerald reminiscence that I could come up with was that back in 1974, when we were interviewing (the now-late) Charles Newman for the chairmanship of our Hopkins Writing Seminars, we lodged him for the night in the "Scott Fitzgerald Apartment" of the old Cambridge Arms, across noisy Charles Street from the university, where Scott had lived while his wife Zelda was being treated at Hopkins's Phipps Psychiatric Clinic and the Sheppard Pratt Hospital; and when I mentioned the next morning that that was also where he'd written much of "The Crack-Up," Newman rolled his ill-slept eyes and said, "I can understand why."

But strange to say, although I knew that biographical datum, I had never read the "Crack-Up" essay/confession that Fitzgerald first published in three *Esquire* installments in 1936—nor did I bother to go read them even after telling that Cambridge Arms anecdote to this organization in 1997. Nor had I lately gone back to read or re-read any of the fiction. And so I accepted tonight's invitation in part to remedy that remissness—*mea maxima culpa!*—and I'm glad I did. Of the fiction, I chose to re-read his precocious first novel, *This Side of Paradise*, which in 1920 launched its young author to fame and fortune and persuaded Zelda to marry him, and which I had first read as an undergraduate wannabe writer myself in the late 1940s. And of the non-fiction, I found in our house library over in

Chestertown and read for the first time a handsome little New Directions Bibelots edition of *The Jazz Age*—and I was wowed.

What most entertained, impressed, and amused me about the *novel* this time through (apart from the story itself) were two things that I hadn't remembered from my first reading of it: the more or less Shakespearian verse-passages that the author opens and closes some chapters with, and the formal novelty of the several one-paragraph sub-chapters: an echo, to my ears, of the formal playfulness of Laurence Sterne and Denis Diderot, and an anticipation of some contemporary "Romantic Formalists," as I call them (including Yours Truly). Here are two examples, a chapter entitled simply "Descriptive," which reads in its entirety:

> Amory was now eighteen years old, just under six feet tall and exceptionally, but not conventionally, handsome. He had rather a young face, the ingenuousness of which was marred by the penetrating green eyes, fringed with long dark eyelashes. He lacked somehow that intense animal magnetism that so often accompanies beauty in men or women; his personality seemed rather a mental thing, and it was not in his power to turn it on and off like a water faucet. But people never forgot his face.

—And the other, also in its entirety, titled simply "Historical":

> The war began in the summer following his freshman year. Beyond a sporting interest in the German

dash for Paris the whole affair failed either to thrill or interest him. With the attitude he might have held toward an amusing melodrama he hoped it would be long and bloody. If it had not continued he would have felt like an irate ticket holder at a prizefight where the principals refused to mix it up.

That was his total reaction.

And of course I was amused and touched by Amory Blaine's remark, in the "Ha-Ha Hortense" chapterlet immediately following that "Historical" one, that unlike Chicago, which Amory calls a Yale town, "In Baltimore, Princeton was home, and one fell in love."

The novel's heavily Romantic poetry-passages I'm not really qualified to appraise, but I was duly impressed by their Shakespearean/Keatsean sound (to my ear, anyhow): e.g., the opening of Chapter Five—

> A fathom deep in sleep I lie
> With old desires, restrained before,
> To clamor lifeward with a cry,
> As dark flies out the graying door;
> And so in quest of creeds to share
> I seek assertive day again . . .
> But old monotony is there:
> Endless avenues of rain.

—followed by a comparably poetical prose-passage which concludes with Amory standing in "The unwelcome November rain [that] had perversely stolen the day's last hour and pawned it with that ancient fence, the night."

Bravo, Scott! Notice that "day," which had been

"assertive" in the preceding poetry-passage, has now become the hapless victim of nasty, thieving rain and of rain's presumably male partner-in-crime, "that ancient fence, the night" (most pawnbrokers are of the male persuasion—with a few notable exceptions, Shelly reminds me, such as Alena Ivanovna in Dostoyevsky's *Crime and Punishment*). We're a long way from Homer's formulaic "Rosy-Fingered Dawn rising from the couch of Night," her presumably male consort in the *Iliad* and *Odyssey*. But by the end of that same rain-splattered chapter, "Night" appears to have been transgendered: In another really over-the-top verse-passage,

> . . . night
> Tears from her wetted breast the splattered blouse
> Of day, glides down the dreaming hills, tear-bright
> To cover with her hair the eerie green . . .

Night is now a (topless) woman; Day is an inanimate messed-up garment—and I, for one, am dizzied by the precocious young author's erratic virtuosity, like a flashy Stutz Bearcat not always under its driver's control.

I'll close with a quick jump from the Roaring Twenties to the Great Depression and a passage from "The Crack-Up" that foreshadows the current state of print-lit as eerily as the 1930s foreshadowed our current economic malaise:

> . . . one by one, [my] convictions were swept away.
> I saw that the novel, which at my maturity was
> the strongest and supplest medium for conveying
> thought and emotion from one human being to

another, was becoming subordinated to a mechanical and communal art that, whether in the hands of Hollywood merchants or Russian idealists, was capable of reflecting only the tritest thought, the most obvious emotion. It was an art in which words were subordinate to images, where personality was worn down to the inevitable low gear of collaboration. As long past as 1930, I had a hunch that the talkies would make even the best selling novelist as archaic as silent pictures. People still read, if only [the] book of the month . . . but there was a rankling indignity, that to me had become almost an obsession, in seeing the power of the written word subordinated to another power, a more glittering, a grosser power . . .

I set that down as an example of what haunted me during the long night [*up in his Cambridge Arms apartment!*]—this was something I could neither accept nor struggle against, something which tended to make my efforts obsolescent, as the chain stores have crippled the small merchant, an exterior force, unbeatable—

And he concludes:

(*I have the sense of lecturing now, looking at a watch on the desk before me and seeing how many more minutes —*).

That closing sentence speaks for me here now as well. Thanks for listening.

LIGHTS OUT

An occasional nuisance in rural areas like our former summer residence on Maryland's Eastern Shore of Chesapeake Bay: either a car hits a utility pole or else a lightning-bolt or an errant squirrel zaps a power transformer, and the electricity goes off for several hours (occasionally, as after some hurricanes, for two or three days). Most of our neighbors had long since installed automatic auxiliary generators to power at least part of the house in those circumstances, but in order to avoid that multi-thousand-dollar outlay, which would also involve some re-landscaping and burying a second propane tank in the front yard, we made shift for three decades with a cumbersome portable rig—awkward to set up and decommission, noisy to operate, and capable of powering only such bare necessities as well pump, basement sump pump, kitchen, and TV/reading-room, and those for only most of the day (we turned the noisy thing off at bedtime). No heat or air conditioning; no working computers or lights in our studies, bedrooms, and bathrooms: we got by with candles and kerosene lamps, flushed the toilets and opened the refrigerator as seldom as possible, lighted the kitchen stove with a gas match normally used to light dinner-table candles, drank instant coffee instead of percolated, caught the news and weather updates on our little portable emergency radio, and drove into town for dinner unless the electricity was off there as well (but some of the restaurants had standby power).

Each time we needed to use that auxiliary generator, with its hazardous exhaust fumes and its cumbersome commissioning and decommissioning, we'd vow to bite the bullet and install an automatic backup. But then the electricity would come back on: we'd shut the generator down, re-set clocks and water-conditioner and pool-filter timers, flush the toilets, thank Thomas Edison and his fellow inventors for their contributions to our comfort—and relapse into procrastination, shaking our heads at how our ancestors got by (and many of our species still manage) without electricity, running water, flush-toilets, and other such basic comforts and conveniences. Bothersome though those temporary power outages were, they moved us—like sprained joints, passing illnesses, and temporary absences of a loved one—to count our blessings and re-appreciate what we tend to take for granted.

Lights out? Let's cuddle!

IN THE DARK
or,
WHY NOT?
(A Zen Koan)

She: How many Zen masters does it take to change a light bulb?

He: Why do you ask?

She: Why do you ask Why do I ask?

He: Why not? Why do *you* ask Why do *I* ask Why do *you* ask?

She: Why not?

He: Shall we change the subject?

She: Why not? I'll change the subject; you change the light bulb.

He: Why not? Better yet, shall we *drop* the subject?

She: Why not?

MY TWO PENS

For many decades, my custom has been to spend mornings at my writing desk, composing—or at least hoping to compose—fiction on Mondays through Thursdays, and essays or other nonfiction on Fridays (hence the titles of my three nonfiction collections: *The Friday Book, Further Fridays*, and *Final Fridays*), first-drafting them in longhand in my seventy-year-old three-ring loose-leaf binder and then typing them into my computer for further editing and printing. Moreover, for some reason or other I've habitually used separate fountain-pens for those first-draft genres: 1) a British Parker 51 bought long ago at a stationery in Rochester, England, that declared itself to be the original of "Mr. Pumblechook's premises" in Charles Dickens's *Great Expectations* and thus led me to call that dear pen Pumblechook and use it for first-drafting my fiction; and 2) a *Meisterstück* bought somewhile later in Stuttgart, Germany, which I use for first-drafting nonfiction on Fridays.

Both pens have served me well for decades; I value them both (with maybe just a little more fondness for Pumblechook) and refill them faithfully with good black ink—so hard to find nowadays in office-supply stores that I half-hope my two-thirds-empty last bottle of Higgins Fountain-Pen India will outlast its late-octogenarian owner. More and more in recent years I've taken to making notes with a *ballpoint* pen and then composing on the computer, but I still relish the flow of fountain-pen ink onto paper, even though my penmanship has declined with age, as has my productivity in both fiction and nonfiction. So it goes—inexorably, but fortunately not in a hurry.

Recently I happened to reread much of Miguel Cervantes's *Don Quixote*, one of my career-long navigation-stars (together with Homer's *Odyssey*, Anonymous's *1001 Nights*, and Mark Twain's *Huckleberry Finn*), and I was especially impressed this time with its *ending*. *DQ* has often been called "the first modern novel"; it could as well be called the first *post*modern novel because of its consciousness of itself. It pretends to be written not by Señor Cervantes, but by "El Cid Hamete Benengeli," who at the novel's close bids *hasta la vista* to the (quill) pen with which he has written it. It's a moving passage, of which I'm reminded more and more as I approach age ninety. I'm not yet ready to "hang up my quill," but at each morning's end, when I turn from longhand drafting to the word-processor, I bid my pen-*du-jour* not *adios*, but *hasta la vista, compadre*, and *muchas gracias!*

THE DESTROYER OF DELIGHTS

"Something I've always admired about our story," old Scheherazade said, closing and setting aside her weathered copy of *Kitab Alf Laylah Wah Laylah*, or *Book of a Thousand Nights and a Night*, "—I mean our *stories?*—is their ending not with some silly-sentimental *happily ever after*, but with the much-more-realistic *until the Destroyer of Delights and Severer of Societies fetched them to the grave and their palaces lay in ruins*, et cetera."

"Yes, well," replied her sister Dunyazade (a.k.a. "Doonie," merely in her seventies, whereas "Sherry" was eighty-plus): "not the happiest of endings, but realistic for sure. This dear place has really gone downhill since our hubbies kicked—or *passed*, as the obituaries like to say. May they R.I.P."

S: Or R.I.H., for all I care: Rot In Hell.

D: You don't miss Shahryar?

S: Are you kidding? The bastard raped and killed a thousand virgins before I came along and pacified him with my stories and a few kinky little tricks I'd learned from the *Kama Sutra*. I'm supposed to *miss* him?

D: But you made him really nice, Sherry. And he gave

116

you three sweet children, which is more than his brother gave me . . .

S: Shah Zaman, *blah*: popped and killed *two* thousand virgins before you cured him. And then went impotent with remorse and gave you no kids. Some *mensch* he was!

D: He had his good qualities. Couldn't get it up, but he was great at going down, and he had a thousand and one little gadgets. I wasn't bored in bed.

S: Okay, so he couldn't bore, but he could tickle. Do you miss him at all?

D: A little, maybe, for sure. Not a lot.

S: Ditto me mine. They had their good qualities, despite their god-awful track record. As for those quote "kids" of mine? In their late fifties now, and scattered all over the map. Ali Shar's still a bachelor; Gharib's married but childless; Jamilah-Melissa is divorced, with grown-up children and no grandchildren. They visit now and then, but I'm not much of a traveler, and caravan-mail takes forever.

D: Doesn't it, though: by the time we get the news, it's history. Rocs and genies were much better carriers than the Shah's postal service.

S: Anyhow, we tale-tellers prefer word of mouth: the Oral Tradition.

D: Better than the Anal, for sure. Speaking of which, that ass-hole Shah Zaman . . .

S: Spare me the details, Sis, and I'll spare you chapter and verse of Shahryar's kinky quirks.

D: Subject dropped. How 'bout a story? Know any good ones?

S: Come off it, Doony: we've heard them all; I've *told* them all. Dreaming up a new story is as likely for us as finding a new way to make love.

D: Which is to say, dot dot dot . . .

S: *Once upon a fucking time there was a fucking story that began . . .*

D: It *has* been a fucking-time, and it *has* been a fucking-story. On with it!

S: Dot dot dot et cetera ad infinitum or ad nauseam, whichever comes first.

D: With us in Samarkand it was nearly always hubby who came first, *tant pis* for me. How was it with you-all?

S: I had a few tricks. Like with my storytelling: finish one, start another, and break off its Rising Action at the crack of dawn, like *coitus interruptus.*

D: . . . ?

S:

THE DIXON LINE

A *Festschrift* tribute to Stephen Dixon (9/25/2018)

It has been my privilege to know Steve Dixon as a person, as a writer, and as a longtime colleague in the Johns Hopkins Writing Seminars. I'll speak briefly here of each of those:

The person: or shall we say *the Mensch*, he being very much that, a high-principled combination of large spirit and New York City smarts: athletic, a prodigiously productive writer, loving husband and father, and impassioned mentor of his lucky students. Like myself, Steve is not a "scholar" in the rigorous-Ph.D. way of most Hopkins faculty (and of his wife, Anne Frydman, a well-credentialed scholar of Russian literature). But he knows whereof he speaks, does Steve, both on the page and in the classroom. His and Anne's happy marriage was tragically cut short by her early death, but blessed by two devoted daughters, adults themselves now and lovingly supportive of their father.

The writer: staggeringly productive, and the product is fiction of consistently high quality. I'm not an *un*productive writer, but compared to Steve's profluence mine is a modest output. And unlike him, I've known a few spells of "writer's block," as it's called in the trade—or "constipation of the Muse," as it's called in my shop. I once mentioned this to Steve, and he advised me when blocked to try writing just *anything* and see what would follow. So when blockage next occurred, I duly wrote on the blank page ANYTHING. Nothing followed, and so after ANYTHING I wrote NOTHING. When nothing followed from *that*, my silent Muse whispered "Enough of this," and heeding her advice I capped my trusty pen, closed my trusty notebook, shut down my trusty computer, and . . . took a walk or a swim, did some chores, read a book, whatever. And *voila*, thank Zeus, in time the block unblocked, at least for a while.

The colleague: a valued one he was, by me and by our department, and in my and his retirement I feel him still to be—an exemplar of attentiveness, productivity, and caring colleaguehood. Bravo, maestro: Anything/Nothing/ On with the story and your stories!

Footnote 11.6.19: Steve Dixon died today in Baltimore, from Parkinson's and pneumonia. Rest in peace, dear colleague—lovingly obituaried in the *New York Times*, *Washington Post*, and *Baltimore Sun*.

BY BARTHELME BEGUILED

(Prefatory note to "Among the Beanwoods" and "Heather"
for The Hopkins Review)

How I've missed, for nearly two decades now, the whimsical, beguiling fictive voice of my near-coeval Donald Barthelme (1931-1989), silenced prematurely by cancer at age fifty-eight. Reviewers and critics often lumped us together (or gave us our lumps), with sundry others, first as Black Humorists, later as Fabulists, finally and most persistingly as Postmodernists. And although I believe that we ourselves were at least as impressed by our muses' differences as by any similarities, we respected one another's stuff and much enjoyed our occasional path-crossings. Don and I exchanged books and shared reading-platforms here and there a number of times; I was his guest at the University of Houston and he mine at Johns Hopkins, where he chatted memorably with the apprentice fictionists in our Writing Seminars.* Indeed, both in conversation and in print I find myself still quoting from time

---

* His two younger brothers Frederick and Steven, published writers with distinctive styles of their own, are both alumni of the Hopkins graduate Seminars.

to time some of his remarks to them on that occasion:
e.g., (here I go again), that the important question to ask
of a piece of fiction isn't whether it's Realist or Irrealist,
Innovative or Traditional, Modernist or Postmodernist or
whatever; the important question, he declared, is "Does
it knock your socks off?" Or his response to the student
who asked how she and her seminar-mates might become
better writers: "Well, for one thing," offered Donald, "you
might try reading all of philosophy, from the pre-Socra-
tics up through last semester." And when the questioner
then good-humoredly protested that I had already advised
them to read all of *literature*, from the Egyptian Middle
Kingdom up through last semester, "That, too," Don
replied: "You're probably wasting time on stuff like eating
and sleeping. Cease that, and go read everything."

Such a fellow! Such a literary voice (primarily, though
by no means exclusively, in the short-story form), enjoyed
not only by aficionados of Serious Lit, but by regular readers of The *New Yorker*, his frequentest venue—and silenced
while still at its peak.

Thanks however to the efforts of *The Hopkins Review*'s
managing editor Glenn Blake—himself a fine fictionist and
former student of both Donald's and mine—two hither-
to-unpublished stories turned up recently in Don's literary
archives, and (with the kind permission of Marion Knox
Barthelme [Donald's widow, and a native Baltimorean]
and his aforementioned brother and literary executor
Frederick Barthelme [director of the Center for Writers
at the University of Southern Mississippi],) they see their
first print here. "Among the Beanwoods" is an enchanting
monologue delivered in an obscurely enchanted place and
situation; "Heather" is the dialogue/trialogue of an infant

girl's father and two street-smart young women who claim to have (jointly) given birth to her . . . Vintage DB, they are: fantastical, sometimes mystifying but always sharply rendered, poignant, and wonderfully entertaining. What a treat, to be by that voice and vision once again beguiled!

Enjoy!

THE IMP OF THE PERVERSE

A *Festschrift* tribute to Robert Coover

Although the label applied to us over the decades kept changing—Fabulists, Black Humorists, Postmodernists—the list of Usual Suspects remained fairly constant: in alphabetical order, John Barth, Donald Barthelme, Robert Coover, William Gaddis, William Gass, John Hawkes, Thomas Pynchon. We ourselves, I believe, were more impressed by the *differences* between our stuff than by what critics and reviewers took to be their similarities, but we respected one another's work and enjoyed one another's company at our occasional path-crossings at some university campus or literary conference. When Bob Coover belatedly joined the ranks of fiction-writing academics by becoming Brown University's (and the planet's) first-ever Professor of Electronic Fiction, his boundless energy and hospitality much facilitated those path-crossings: not long after his appointment, he organized a gathering of those Usual Suspects under the Barthelmeish heading *Unspeakable Practices, Unnatural Acts*—the first of several such get-togethers under his auspices.

"Electronic literature?" I remember asking him. "What's that?"

"Check it out," he advised. I did, and while I remained (and remain) a pen-and-ink, printed-page person, for whom the computer is a handy office tool, not a literary medium, I was impressed enough by his Thinking Outside the Box to become an official (though passive) advisor to the Electronic Literature Organization. Bob too, as far as I know, did not himself practice what he took so energetic an interest in. To *think* outside the box is not necessarily to *go* there: his impish, always-lively *oeuvre* consists of printed pages.

Impish, yes: from his earliest novel (*The Origin of the Brunists*, winner of the 1966 PEN/Faulkner award for best first novel of that year) through his recentest as of this writing (*Going for a Beer*, 2018), his signature mode has been the Bad-Boy wink. Some years ago, when a reviewer characterized one of his novels as "unremittingly malevolent," its author was delighted.

The Peck's Bad Boy of Postmodernism? The PoMo Puck? Take your pick.

Abrazos, Comrade Coover!

LIBRARIES

*(Address delivered at the dedication of Alaska's Anchorage
Public Library in 1986, subsequently mislaid in my files,
recently re-found, and here published for the first time.)*

The great contemporary Argentine writer Jorge Luis
Borges, who died just a few months ago (June 14, 1986),
describes *money* in one of his stories as "a collection of
possible futures." That's the way I feel about libraries.

So for that matter did Señor Borges, who for a time
was a librarian himself in Buenos Aires: another of his
stories, called "The Library of Babel," involves an infinite
library, whose innumerable volumes contain every possible combination of alphabetical characters. Such a library
would therefore include not only the record of "actual" past
history, but the record of all imaginable past histories; it
would contain not only the true prediction of the future,
but, alas, the prediction of every possible future. I say "alas"
because in such a library as Borges's imaginary Library of
Babel we would have no way of distinguishing, before the
fact, the accurate prediction from all the slightly or grossly
inaccurate ones. The truth would be there, somewhere, but

126

only chance or special dispensation would lead us to it.

That is the case, metaphorically speaking, with all libraries, despite the best efforts of the most knowledgeable and sophisticated staff, for the reason that every general library represents—indeed, it more or less contains—the accumulated resources of civilization. In the granary of the past are the seeds of the future: the best way to assure a good crop is to make those seeds as accessible as possible to as many as possible.

I shall now wax personal for the space of four paragraphs:

Whatever literary education I have, I got at least as much from random wandering through the libraries of my youth as from the efforts of my official teachers. My hometown in tidewater Maryland in the 1930s was small, southern, semirural, and economically depressed; neither its public-school libraries nor the main county library was anything to crow about, and the librarians were well-meaning but unimaginative sorts who steered all the girls to Nancy Drew and the Bobbsey Twins and all the boys to Tom Swift and the Hardy Boys. Anything more daring I suspect they squirreled away out of our random reach, if they had it at all. Even so, in high-school days, while our official reading kept to the solid but unexciting ground of Walter Scott's *Ivanhoe* and Tennyson's *Idylls of the King*, I somehow stumbled onto Faulkner and Hemingway and Dos Passos in the library, and without quite knowing what I was reading, I commenced my education in modernity.

After high school, I drifted into the Johns Hopkins University on a partial scholarship, quite unprepared for that or any other excellent college. I spent the next few years treading academic water, barely keeping afloat, and though a number of my undergraduate professors were inspiring teachers as well as celebrated scholars, much of my education was *a la carte*.

The "carte" in this case was the book-cart that I pushed for two years through the stacks of the main university library to help defray my tuition costs. It was the university's benign policy, I believe, to employ more student book-filers than were really needed to return borrowed volumes to the library shelves. We work-study people checked in, picked up our loaded carts, and disappeared into the stacks, under no pressure to reappear soon. My territory happened to be the stacks of classical Greek and Roman literature and of William Foxwell Albright's Oriental Seminary, which contained classical Egyptian, Persian, Arabic, Hebrew, and Sanskrit literature; I made frequent expeditions as well into the stacks of the modern European languages. Much of what I filed was in the original, all Greek to me, but plenty of it was in translation, and I not only shamelessly read while I was working, but often borrowed what I was supposed to be re-shelving. I immersed myself in (but did not study) Homer, Aeschylus, Sophocles, Euripides, Aristophanes, Herodotus, Virgil, Ovid, Petronius, Catullus, and hosts of lesser classical fry; also in the Egyptian *Book of the Dead*, the Persian/Arabian *Thousand and One Nights*, the Sanskrit *Panchatantra*, and *Kama Sutra* and *Vetalapanchavimsati* (which I still remember means *Twenty-five Tales Told by a Vampire*), and in such later tale-cycles as the *Decameron*, the *Pentameron*, and the *Heptameron*. If there had existed a *Multimilliameron*, I would have read it from end to end as I shelved its abundant volumes.

My memory of this experience is summed up by the

title of one of those enormous works: the eleventh-century Sanskrit *Kathasaritsagara*, called in English *The Ocean of Story*. To be sure, the library comprised other oceans as well, just as the planet does: the ocean of history, the oceans of the several sciences, the arts, etc.. But it was my prolonged, weightless immersion in the ocean of ancient storytelling that gestated me into a storyteller myself and marinated my imagination for keeps. Much as I have to thank my various teachers and coaches for (not to mention such extracurricular instructors as parents, siblings, lovers, spouses, children, colleagues, friends, even enemies), my main thanks, when I'm in the thanking rather than the blaming mode, goes to the library. I encourage the apprentice writers in my charge to follow their old coach's example in this particular: Go get yourselves happily lost in that treasure-house, the way you get lost in a good dictionary. When you've found the book you thought you were looking for, poke round a bit to the right and then left of it, the shelves above and the shelves below, also the next alcove over and the one around the corner. You may serendipitously find the book you were really looking for without knowing it: the keys to the treasury of your own imagination.

To come back to that late lamented spellbinder Jorge Luis Borges: the hero of yet another of his stories is a Czechoslovakian writer named Jaromir Hladík, condemned to death by the Nazis for the crime of being partly Jewish. On his last night on earth, Hladík prays for time to complete his unfinished play, and toward dawn he has a crucial dream:

... he dreamt he had hidden himself in one of the

naves of the Clementine Library. A librarian wearing dark glasses asked him: What are you looking for? Hladík answered: God. The librarian told him, God is in one of the letters on one of the pages of one of the 400,000 volumes of the Clementine. My fathers and the fathers of my fathers have sought after that letter. I've gone blind looking for it. He removed his glasses, and Hladík saw that his eyes were dead. A reader came to return an atlas. This atlas is useless, he said, and handed it to Hladík, who opened it at random. As if through a haze, he saw a map of India. With a sudden rush of assurance, he touched one of the tiniest letters. An ubiquitous voice said: The time for your work has been granted. Hladík awoke."

The story in which this dream occurs is called "The Secret Miracle"; it has a magnificent ending, which I won't give away. I exhort those of you who don't know it to look it up, here in your splendid new library. Do not let the circulation staff look it up for you; go into the stacks yourself, with only the most general directions, and do not rush to the correct address. Stroll the neighborhood; see what catches your eye. Most of the old Alaskan gold-prospectors didn't find the literal gold they were after; what they found instead was something more interesting: Alaska. You are not likely to find God in the stacks of the Anchorage Public Library, though stranger things have happened. What you might just possibly find is yourself.

"IT'S ALL GREEK TO ME": ANSWERS WITHOUT QUESTIONS

In 2012, during a tourist visit to Greece, I did an interview with Elias Maglinis, editor of the Athens daily newspaper KathImerini. Recently I found in my files my responses to his interview questions—questions that I trust can be inferred from these replies.

Taking your good questions in order, Mr. Maglinis:

1) After jazz-drumming through my high-school years with a group of friends for pleasure and spending-money, in 1947 I enrolled in Juilliard's summer program to study "arranging" (as it was called back in those big-swing-band days), and learned that whatever talent I had in that line was less than I had hoped. So I swallowed hard, came home, went to Johns Hopkins on scholarship, and stumbled into fiction-writing instead, for which I came to feel a true Vocation even though I had everything to learn. But I continued "arranging" and playing drums in dance-bands all through college and beyond, to supplement my teaching salary as well as for the pleasure of it. And as a writer,

I still enjoy taking a received "melody"—a classical myth, say, or a literary convention like Scheherazade's stories-in-a-frame—and "re-orchestrating" it in a new key.

2 & 3) Good questions—but who can reply, except retrospectively (another kind of reorchestration)? I cut my apprentice teeth on the great Modernists—Faulkner, Joyce, Kafka, Mann, Proust—along with the "traditional" tale-tellers like Homer, Scheherazade, and Boccaccio, and the early convention-defying novelists like Rabelais, Laurence Sterne, and Diderot. Over the decades, my own fiction has been classified as Existentialist, Black Humorist, Fabulist, Post-Modernist . . . Such category-labels can be useful when discussing art or anything else, but I finally shrug my shoulders and get on with it, never quite knowing what my muse will do next: a sort of low-grade suspense that keeps me going from project to project . . .

4) More Categories! In fact (at my work-table, at least) whatever happens happens: a project may hatch from an image, a character, a "theme," a story-idea: sometimes the "world-view" gives rise to the story, sometimes vice versa.

5) I don't "aim," as a rule: I just shoot. Prevailingly, my muse has been the one with the grin instead of the grimace; but she switches masks from time to time, or combines them.

6) "Optimistic," "pessimistic" . . . I agree with my late literary comrade Donald Barthelme that the important question to ask of a work of fiction isn't whether it's Optimistic or Pessimistic, Realist or Irrealist, Traditional

or Innovative; the important question is "Is it first-rate?" Or, as Barthelme put it, "Does it knock your socks off?" (What would be the comparable idiom in Greek?)

7) I've never felt that the Novel as a literary genre was Kaput. What my "Literature of Exhaustion" essay addressed was the widespread feeling, back in the 1960s, that it *might* be, and how that climate of opinion might itself inspire lively new work—as Jorge Luis Borges so artfully demonstrated.

8) That's a brilliant constellation of writers, with whom it's an honor to be associated whether one deserves to be or not. But as usual when I see such listings, I'm at least as impressed by their *dissimilarities* as by any similarities among them. The particular importance to me of discovering Borges back in the 1960s was that up until then I'd been exclusively a novel-writer. His *Fictions* re-awakened my interest in the short-story form and inspired my "*Lost in the Funhouse*" series and the "*Chimera*" novella-triad. I still think of myself as mainly a novelist by temperament, but now and then I enjoy returning to the short forms—as I'm doing currently.

9) Philip Roth is probably correct, alas, thanks to the distractions of television, video games, and other electronic diversions: my colleagues at Johns Hopkins tell me that even their fiction-writing students are much less widely read than they used to be, although they turn out page after page of their own fiction! So it may be that literary readership is going the way of our planet's rain forests and coral reefs. More likely, the novel and short story are

becoming ever more a "special niche" pleasure, like poetry since the nineteenth century. Better that than extinction!

10) My "Islam," for better or worse, is the Islam of "*The Thousand and One Nights*"; my contact with contemporary Islam has been negligible. I did have the interesting experience years ago of delivering in Morocco my lecture on Scheherazade's menstrual cycle as a (half-serious) key to *The 1001 Nights*—to a mixed audience of locals and American students, in an outdoor lecture theater on the last night of Ramadan, with the crescent moon rising over nearby minarets like the very flag of Islam—and wondering whether I might be giving great unintended offense! But several women Arab-literature scholars in the audience assured me that they found the talk amusing and even enlightening—and that the *Nights* were not regarded as Serious Literature anyhow. Very courteous of them! My heartfelt thanks, by the way, to the novelist Alexis Panselinos and to (the translator of "*Somebody the Sailor*") for their rendition of some of my writings into Greek. Robert Frost famously defined poetry as "that which gets lost in translation"—but I wonder sometimes whether prose can perhaps gain in translation? A pleasant possibility.

11) Like most of our American friends, neighbors, and colleagues, my wife and I are appalled and embarrassed by both the foreign and the domestic policies of the current US presidency, in particular our disastrous war in Iraq. One hopes for more enlightened presidencies down the road, but it's hard to resist the Tragic View of history (a Greek invention, as I recall). *Epharisto!*

OUT OF THE CRADLE

"I stand here ironing," declares the narrator of Tillie Olsen's much-anthologized short story of that title. Me, I sit here rocking—in my two-dozen-year-old swivel desk chair at my forty-plus-year-old worktable, between strokes of my Parker (19)51 fountain pen in the seventy-year-old loose-leaf binder (picked up during my freshman orientation at Johns Hopkins in 1947) in which I've first-drafted every apprentice and then professional sentence of my writing life, up to and including this extended one—my now nearly nine-decades-old body taking idle comfort in the so-familiar oscillation that has, this workday morning, caught the attention of its octogenarian mind.

Nothing vigorous, this rocking: just a gentle, intermittent back-and-forthing as I scan my notes and exfoliate them into these sentences and paragraphs. Notes, e.g., on the ubiquitous popularity of rocking chairs (including the iconic John F. Kennedy Rocker), porch swings, hammocks, and the like: a popularity surely owing to our body's memory of having been calmed and soothed through babyhood in parental arms, cradles, infant-slings, maybe, later on, rocking-horses. And in adulthood, a particularly delicious feeling for my wife and myself was the gentle rocking of our cruising sailboat at anchor in one of the many snug coves of Chesapeake Bay. These calmative effects in turn no doubt derive from our prenatal rocking in the womb as our mothers went about their pregnant daily business, themselves rocking in chairs now and then to rest between stand-up chores and to lull their increasingly active cargo. We are not surprised to hear from neuroscientists and physicians that rocking releases endorphins, which abet our physical and mental health—though one also remembers the furious, feverish rocking of the never-to-be-soothed protagonist in D. H. Lawrence's ironically titled "The Rocking-Horse Winner."

Old-timers, especially, favor rockers as they circle toward second childhood, and nursing homes, particularly ones for patients with dementia, are more and more using rocking chairs as therapy: thus from "Rock-a-Bye Baby" we rock and roll our way to Hoagy Carmichael's "Old Rockin' Chair's Got Me." "Out of the cradle, endlessly rocking," writes Walt Whitman of the waves of Long Island Sound, "I . . . a reminiscence sing." A boyhood beach-memory, it is, of his having sharply pitied the keenings of a male mockingbird bereft of its mate: desolated love-cries that the Good Gray Poet is pleased in retrospect to imagine having inspired his whole ensuing poetical life's work. And that he now "fuses" with the sea's "low and delicious word"—"Death, death, death, death, death"—to arrive at an intellectual acceptance and emotional transcendence of The End. Not for us to question whether, in Whitman's case, the poem's conclusion declares a psychological accomplishment on its author's part or merely raises a hopeful/wishful possibility.

In my own case, as befits a mere novelist, the out-of-the cradle rocking-reminiscence is more prosaic: for the first seventeen-and-then-some years of my life—from babyhood until college—it was my fixed nightly habit to rock myself to sleep. Left-side down in bed, I would roll gently back and forth into oblivion at a rate slightly lower (so I've just confirmed by comparing kinesthetic memory, surprisingly strong, with my watch's sweep-second hand) than my once-per-second normal pulse. About 1.5 seconds per rock it was, by my present reckoning, or forty rocks per minute—which I now further discover to approximate my most natural-feeling frequency for desk-and rocking-chair rocking as well. Try it yourself, reader: Once per second feels frenetic, no? And once every *second* second a bit laggard? When "restive" (odd adjective, that; it sounds as if it ought to mean rest-*conducive* rather than rest-*resistant*), I would rock even in partial sleep.

So I learned from my twin sister, whom my habit never seemed to bother in the ten or so prepubescent years when we shared a bedroom (with, appropriately, twin beds); perhaps she was inured to it from our months together in the womb. And so I was reminded further and less patiently by my older brother in the several subsequent years of our room-sharing, between my puberty and his departure for college and military service, through which interval I troubled his repose with my rockrockrocking and he mine in turn, more intriguingly (if I ceased rocking and feigned sleep), with the soft slapslap of adolescent masturbation, which his kid brother was only just discovering. And so I was reminded finally by the teasing of college roommates, who pretended to think I must be jerking off in some exotic wise when, too ashamed at that age and stage to rock myself to sleep, I sometimes embarrassed myself and entertained them by endlessly rocking in my sleep.

An old-time Freudian, one supposes, would maintain that it was in fact masturbative, that rhythmic back-and-forthing that wore away the shoulder of my teenage pajamas from friction against the bed-sheets. But hey: masturbation as far back as pre-Kindergarten? Sure, our hypothetical Freudian would reply: all toddlers play with their privates until shamed out of doing so, whereupon the instinctual itch finds other outlets, or inlets. Yes, well, maybe: but about my rocking as a mode of post-pubescent-though-still-virginal Getting It Off, I feel the way Robert Frost felt about his critics' reading his "Stopping by Woods on a Snowy Evening" as a poem about the death-wish: "When I write a poem about death," Frost maintained in effect, "I write a poem about death. When I want to write about stopping by woods on a snowy evening, I write about that." Or, more directly to the point, the young woman in one of Bruno Bettelheim's classes whose fiddling with her hair during his lectures reputedly so distracted the eminent psychiatrist that he admonished her publicly by declaring that what she was doing was a sublimated form of masturbation—to which she spiritedly replied, "When I feel like masturbating, Dr. Bettelheim, I masturbate. When I fiddle with my hair, I'm fiddling with my hair." By age fourteen, when I was inclined to whack off I whacked off. Rocking myself to sleep was a different business altogether.

Which is not to deny any twenty-first-century holdout's contention that even to the busily copulative and/or explicitly masturbatory, the gratification of rocking in bed—yea, even of rocking in desk chair or front-porch rocker—may have a mild erotic component. If so, however, then like

reflexology or floating on gentle sea-waves (in my experience of giving or indulging those pleasures, at least), it's
more assuaging than arousing to the carnal itch—rather
like "shuckling," the Jewish custom of swaying back and
forth while reciting the Torah. Anyhow, as a wise philos-
ophy-professor used to remind us Hopkins undergrads,
one arrives at generality only by ignoring enough partic-
ularity: the more a proposition applies to everything in
general, the less it applies to anything in particular. If my
real subject were erotic gratification, I'd be "off my rocker"
to write about rocking myself into the arms of Morpheus
in bedtime years of yore and, in desk chair work-mornings
since, into fruitful intercourse with the muse.

Right?

Not quite right, in this context, that old slang expres-
sion for "crazy"—which my *Pocket Dictionary of American
Slang* dates to circa 1930 (the year of my and my sister's birth) but gives no derivation of, as does neither my
American Heritage Dictionary nor my compact *O.E.D.*
To be "off one's rocker" sounds turn-of-last-century
mechanical to me, in the vein more of "slipped one's trol-
ley" than of a senseless "out of one's chair." In any event,
my infantile habit disappeared, rather swiftly and pain-
lessly as I recall, during that freshman college year, thus
sparing me the embarrassment that I used to fear more
than my roommate's teasing: that I might unconsciously
fall to rocking while sleeping with a woman when that
eagerly-anticipated time arrived, and frighten the bejesus
out of her. And there've been no relapses in the decades
since, although even nowadays my wife will sometimes ask
me please to quit distracting her by rocking in my chair
when we're reading or TV-watching in a room together.

Recliners I can do without, but if there's a rocker I'll go for it, and only with some effort eschew its intended function.

Meanwhile, back on campus, this then-new old loose-leaf binder was filling up with lecture notes and term-paper drafts, its divider tabs labeled EUR HIST, LIT CLASSICS, POL SCI, and the like, instead of their present W[ork] I[n]P[rogress]#1, WIP#2, etc.—the former for front-burner fiction in the works, the latter for essays, lectures, and such miscellanies as this. By sophomore year I had managed to get myself duly and rockinglessly laid and had amended those notebook-dividers, replacing JOURN[alism], my tentative original major, with something like FICT 101. The exact name of the university's introductory fiction-writing course escapes me (Hopkins's brand-new degree-granting creative writing program was one of only two such in the nation back then; nowadays, for better or worse, there are above 400), but not the trial-and-error pleasures of fumbling my way into Vocation.

In those green semesters of literary (and, coincidentally, sexual) apprenticeship, did I have a swivel-rocking chair? Not impossibly, although it and the desk it served will have been among the battered Goodwill Industries cheapos wherewith we-all furnished our off-campus student-warren row-house walk-ups. What strikes me now—what nudges my patient Parker 51, anyhow—is that it will have been just about when I ceased rocking myself to sleep that I awoke to my calling and commenced my curriculum vitae as a desk-chair-rocking Writer (and, coincidentally, lover/husband/father). What had formerly been a sedative, a tranquilizing soporific, had morphed into a facilitator of reflection, contemplation, deliberation, even inspiration: in both aspects, one supposes, a channeler and discharger of mild but maybe mildly distracting nervous energy.

So? Sixty years on, a veteran wordsmith now and a seasoned octogenarian, I find my musings sometimes preoccupied with that latter datum and, by obvious extension, with my mortality: a preoccupation that, while often sharpening the pleasures of a many-blessinged life, sometimes dulls their edge and threatens to pre-empt my professional imagination. Unlike Walt Whitman, I do not find "the sea's low word" delicious and reconciliatory, much less inspiring; I find it quietly chilling. Death (and worse, one's own and one's mate's approaching infirmity, dependency, bereavement, and the rest) *inspiring*? One would have to be . . . *off one's rocker* to find it so! Or else believe in some Happy Hereafter—which I utterly cannot.

How then come to terms with The End, except—small comfort, but doubtless better than none—by fashioning sentences, paragraphs, pages out of its inexorable approach, while not for a moment imagining that such wordsmithery will delay by even 1.5 seconds the thing's arrival?

I rock and consider, in pensive (though not wordless) vain . . .

ON HAVING NOTHING
FURTHER TO SAY

P.S.

. . . ?